# Live Your Life
—— for ——
# Half the Price

*Also by Lyle and Tracy Shamo*
DEBT-FREE ON ANY INCOME

# Live Your Life
## —— for ——
# Half the Price

## LYLE AND TRACY SHAMO

DESERET
BOOK

SALT LAKE CITY, UTAH

For more ideas on thrifty living,
visit www.live4half.com

DESERET BOOK is a registered trademark of Deseret Book Company.

Visit us at DeseretBook.com

**Library of Congress Cataloging-in-Publication Data**

Shamo, Lyle.
  Live your life for half the price / Lyle Shamo and Tracy Shamo.
    p.  cm.
  Includes bibliographical references and index.
  ISBN 978-1-60641-145-2 (paperbound)
  1. Finance, Personal—United States.  I. Shamo, Tracy.  II. Title.
  HG179.S4285 2009
  332.02400973—dc22
                                                          2009026180

Printed in the United States of America
Artistic Printing, Salt Lake City, UT

10    9    8    7    6    5    4    3    2    1

*The three essentials to achieve anything are, first, hard work;*
*second, stick-to-itiveness; third, common sense.*
*—Thomas Edison*

# Contents

# Contents

# A Penny Saved
# Is a Penny Earned

How often do you walk through a parking lot and find a penny staring up at you? If a penny falls from a pocket, no one misses it, right? But one hundred pennies add up to a dollar, five hundred to five dollars, and one thousand to ten dollars. The secret to living life on less is to realize that every "penny saved is a penny earned."

The Humphrey family from Staten Island, New York, knows just how quickly pennies can add up. That realization started in October 2005 when Barbara Humphrey spotted a nickel and two pennies lying on the ground while waiting for a college class to start. She went home that night and decided to start a little blog about finding change. The next day she found a dime and recorded it on her blog site. Soon her husband, Scott, an army sergeant, and their two daughters started to collect small change as well.

The Humphreys placed their coins in a bank fashioned from a votive candleholder. When the coins became too many for the bank, the family expanded their savings into a pretzel jar. By the end of the year, the coins nearly filled a five-gallon water jug. In three years they had collected from the streets of New York a little more than $1,000, proving that a penny saved truly is a penny earned.[1]

We began a similar process early in our marriage that still

continues. It began with a family home evening lesson on saving money. We found an empty peanut butter jar, washed it, placed it on a bookshelf, and began to deposit any loose change into the jar. When one jar became full, we began to fill a second jar. Over the years we grew quite a coin collection. The payoff came three years later, just after the birth of our first baby. She was born prematurely and was very sick. We stayed up night after night with her walking the floor. One night, utterly exhausted, we both realized that something had to be done. We decided we needed to buy a rocking chair, but we had no extra cash and didn't know where we were going to get enough money. It was then that we looked up and spotted the change in the jars. Would it be enough? Eagerly we opened the jars and began to count the coins. We were surprised to find that we had saved enough money to cover the cost of a rocking chair, with five dollars left over. It was a miracle! Pennies *do* add up.

A friend told us that he had received his education on the value of a dollar from his first job, working at a gravel pit. He hated it! The work was backbreaking. He was always hot, sweaty, and dirty. The worst part was that the big, noisy machinery caused every bone in his body to rattle. On his days off he would often encounter opportunities to spend his hard-earned cash. The image of the gravel pit, however, was always with him. When he saw a movie he wanted to see or a shirt he liked or something more expensive he wanted to buy, he would always ask himself the same question as he ran a few calculations in his head: "Is that worth an hour, two hours, or perhaps three days of work in the gravel pit?" That would be the determining factor in making his decision. Most often he would conclude that the object in question simply did not warrant that many hours at his dreadful job. The lessons he learned during that period of time have stayed with him throughout his life. He has always been careful to spend his money wisely.

# We Are Rich

We tend to think the world is a prosperous place with only rare exceptions. Our bounty has skewed reality. The United Nations has a definition for poverty—earning less than a dollar a day. Under the U.N. definition, no one in the United States lives in poverty. But there are 6 billion people in the world, and 1.3 billion of them live on less than a dollar a day; 3 billion live on less than two dollars a day. Add it up—that's more than half the world's population!

Let's look at just how rich *you* are. The World Bank Development Research Group calculated the average worldwide annual income to be $5,000 per year. The accompanying chart shows the yearly income in percentage for different income groups:

| Percentage of world population | Percentage of world income | Yearly individual income | Daily individual income |
|---|---|---|---|
| Bottom 10% | 0.8 | $401 | $1.10 |
| Bottom 20% | 2.0 | $500 | $1.37 |
| Bottom 50% | 8.5 | $850 | $2.33 |
| Bottom 75% | 22.3 | $1,486 | $4.07 |
| Bottom 85% | 37.1 | $2,183 | $5.98 |
| Top 10% | 50.8 | $25,400 | $69.59 |
| Top 5% | 33.7 | $33,700 | $92.33 |
| Top 1% | 9.5 | $47,500 | $130.14 |

Let's put these statistics into perspective. If you earn $50,000 a year, the average U.S. income, then you are among the richest 98 percent of the world. There are billions of people who do not even reach the top 1 percent of wage earners.[2] This means that even if you're in debt, even if your income never meets your expenses, you are still rich. If you have choices about what you will buy, what you will eat, and what you will wear, you are rich! But you can be rich and still be living beyond your means.

# The Poverty of Living beyond Our Means

There is a second kind of poverty: the poverty of living beyond your means. Jean Chatzky of NBC's *Today Show* and *Money* magazine wrote:

> You may think you're living within your means. Four out of five people do. They say no matter how little money they made they'd find a way to live within their means.
>
> But here's the thing. Two out of those five are wrong. They're deceiving themselves, pulling the wool over their own eyes. How do I know? More than half can't afford to pay off their credit cards each month. Only one-third have enough stashed away to weather a financial hardship. Fewer still have enough to save sufficiently for college for their kids and for their own retirement.
>
> Why the disconnect? Because many people don't understand what it is to live within their means. That phrase—and I grant you it's thrown around a lot—means that you are living on your own nut. You are able to afford the life you're living—from the house or apartment you inhabit, to the clothes you buy, the vacations you take, the restaurants you frequent—on your own. You aren't taking money from your parents, and you aren't floating your fun on a credit card.
>
> Six out of ten Americans—singles more than couples, [Generation] Xers more than seniors—don't fit that definition. They're spending more than they can afford on at least one thing and often more than one.[3]

Every family dreams a familiar dream. They believe that if they work hard enough they can obtain a better life for their children. In the turbulent present, some have begun to wonder if this dream is a pipe dream. National statistics are not encouraging. News analysts paint a picture of ever-increasing pressure and mounting skepticism. In the first four years of this century, real median income declined by 3 percent, and the percentage of middle-income households (earning from $25,000 to $99,000) declined by 1.5 percent. At the same time, savings shrank (Americans saved at the lowest rate in seventy-three years), and consumer debt, including credit card balances, soared to an all-time high—approximately $9,312 per household. In addition, health care costs soared through the roof. Fifty-one percent of employees saw an increase in health care costs or received a cut to their health benefits. Another 83 percent said there was little money remaining after paying bills each month. Little wonder that 66 percent of Americans admitted to pollsters that they were living paycheck to paycheck. Almost half told analysts that no matter how hard they worked, they could not get ahead.[4]

We live in a society where everyone wants the newest and the best—car, house, computer, clothing, and on and on. We feel somehow cheated when we have less than the people who live around us. Buying and acquiring things has become *the* way of life. *Now* is the time to change this way of thinking.

## Time or Money

Every choice we make to strike a balance between our income and our expenses involves either time or money. We need time to cut our expenses and improve our income. We can make all our own meals and cut out all prepackaged products. We can grow a garden, read the sales ads, cut coupons, or sell on eBay. This involves time. When we want more money, we have fewer choices. The only way to obtain more money is to get more employment. It is either time or money or both.

What happens in our personal life is only a microcosm of what happens in the world. Whether we face an economic downturn or a personal crisis, it is time to put ourselves on a financial diet. We must prioritize our expenses, patronize discount stores instead of trendy malls, find cheap alternatives to name brands, and make our own meals instead of eating out. In short, we must spend less and save more. No longer can we survive by being slaves to the latest trends. The new style *is* to live on less. We will soon see, to our total amazement, that the simple life is far more rewarding than the indulgent one was. Time becomes money and money becomes time.

# Find the Waste

Just as coins in a jar add up, so do small purchases. It's the little things, not the big ones, that have caused our excesses and sent us so heavily into debt. These purchases may have once seemed to be of no consequence, but they can cause our financial downfall. Financial experts say we waste 16–23 percent of each month's paycheck. That is a lot of pennies.

Only a rare family never wastes a dime. This exceptional breed cherishes each dollar and accounts for every penny. It was probably some past necessity that taught them this valuable lesson. To keep from wasting money, such households undoubtedly grow much of their own food, cook their own meals, and never eat out. Perhaps they even hang their clothes on a line to dry instead of placing them in a clothes dryer. They buy sensible cars to drive to school, church, and work, and they have never been devotees of fashion. If you are one of these rare people, we aren't worried about you. In tough times, you will survive.

The odds are much greater, however, that you fall into the larger group that has not discovered the waste in its budget. Even if you can find only $10 to $15 worth of savings here and there, reading this book will have been worthwhile.

*Live Your Life for Half the Price* was written as a companion piece to our first book, *Debt-Free on Any Income.* The principles in both books are the same. To live a full life on less, you must systematically pay off your debts, and you do that by making a spending plan, tracking it, and adjusting it wherever necessary to find needed funds.

Let's illustrate how this works with a real-life experience. One day a man came to his bishop. He was discouraged over his financial situation. He was a hard worker, but his paycheck didn't keep pace with the demands of his growing family.

"There's absolutely nothing I can do, Bishop," he said. "I can't make it another year."

The bishop replied, "Perhaps there is more you can do than you realize." He then asked the man to describe a typical day. "Where do you go? What do you do? What do you buy?"

"I hope you aren't suggesting that we are not careful," he said. "I can assure you that my wife and I are doing all we can to keep expenses to a minimum."

"Indulge me," the wise bishop said. "Take this pen and paper and write down for me everything you buy in just one week."

The man agreed. At the end of the week, he reported back, his list in hand. Together he and the bishop looked over his expenses. One thing stood out because it happened daily. Each morning before reporting to his construction job, the man stopped by the local convenience store for treats—a few cookies, a big drink, and a couple of candy bars. At lunch he returned for a refill, and on his way home, when he was absolutely famished, he stopped a third time.

"Do you think you could cut down on those trips to the convenience store?" the bishop asked.

"Bishop, you don't know what you are asking. This is how I keep going."

"Try it for one month. Cut your trips to one a day, and see how much you save."

The man left shaking his head, but he tried the experiment. In one month he had saved $300. He could scarcely believe it.

"Now," said the bishop, "take your $300 and begin to pay off your debt. Do it this month and the next month and the month after that."

Whether you are in the process of paying your debts or have already paid them off, you can still make cuts in your expenses that you will never miss. It doesn't take heaps of money to live a full life; it takes only pennies. We hope we can make a believer of you. Times may look bleak, but sunshine is ahead. Ben Franklin was right. A penny saved is—and always will be—a penny earned.

# PART ONE

# The Pursuit of Happiness

# Chapter 1

# The Secret to Living on Less

It is no surprise that we must begin to examine far more closely than we have ever done before the way we spend our money. Whether we have lost a job, worry that we might lose a job, or anticipate a job loss to someone we love, we know we are in a situation where every penny must count. In some way we will all be affected by the encroaching storm, some more significantly than others. No one likes to suffer, and no one likes to see others suffer. With significant losses to people's retirement savings, massive layoffs, and the media's daily tally of failing businesses, a significant number of people are beginning to lose heart. We desire to infuse in you hope sufficient to weather the storm.

Learning to live on less is an art that requires knowledge, training, and practice. Just as a novice pianist cannot immediately play a Rachmaninov concerto, a novice spender cannot immediately make sound fiscal decisions every time he spends his money. Yet we sometimes become discouraged because we feel we are doing everything we can possibly do, and we simply cannot make ends meet. We want you to know that after thirty-seven years of marriage and trying to manage a large family, *we* are still learning. None of us has yet mastered this art. We all make mistakes, and we all have something new to learn.

Fiscal discipline is comparable to the laws of the gospel. The parallels are uncanny. The Lord said:

"Wherefore, verily I say unto you that all things unto me are spiritual, and not at any time have I given unto you a law which was temporal; neither any man, nor the children of men; neither Adam, your father, whom I created. Behold, I gave unto him that he should be an agent unto himself; and I gave unto him commandment, but no temporal commandment gave I unto him, for my commandments are spiritual; they are not natural nor temporal, neither carnal nor sensual" (D&C 29:34–35). If all things are spiritual, then the Lord has provided us with sufficient laws to govern even our financial affairs. In that spirit, let us outline for you some financial principles incorporated under spiritual laws:

1. Live by faith.
2. Let virtue garnish your thoughts.
3. Cultivate a spirit of charity.
4. Organize and prepare yourself.
5. Seek for wisdom, not riches.

# Live by Faith

Faith and fear cannot coexist. Faith causes action; fear causes inaction. "Believing we can" allows us all to survive even under the most perilous conditions. It has always been so. The scriptures are replete with economic stories that revolve around faith.

Joseph in the Old Testament faced bondage twice, spending a great portion of his life enslaved because of gross injustice. But Joseph's ability to interpret dreams, which came as a result of his faith, is what delivered not just him but also his family and all of Egypt from what could have been a catastrophe.

Four hundred years later, descendants of Joseph and his brothers faced bondage. This time it was Moses' faith that pulled them through. Not only did Moses have to deliver his people from their

Egyptian taskmasters, but he also had to deliver them from harsh conditions in the world's largest desert. For forty years, their economic condition was in the hands of the Lord, who worked through his prophet. Moses' faith resulted in the blessings of the Lord. The Lord sent manna and quail to sustain his people, and he always delivered them to sources of fresh water, even if it had to be brought forth by Moses striking his staff against a rock. Ultimately the people were delivered to a promised land.

Other prophets faced similar adversity and survived by their faith. Banished to a wilderness, Elijah was fed by ravens. Elisha, his successor, was delivered from starvation by a widow who fed him with the last crumbs of her meal (1 Kings 17:8–16). Her faith also reaped a profit, for the barrel of meal never ran out. Lehi's family fled the comfort of Jerusalem and survived a harsh environment before their arrival in America. Even the loss of their only bow was handled through the exercise of faith. The resilient sons of Helaman were taught by their mothers to never doubt. They faced armies and came perilously close to destruction, yet not one of them perished (Alma 56:27, 60). Faith can carry us through tough economic conditions.

In our own day we have prophets who can deliver us in the exact same manner. Recall the words President Gordon B. Hinckley delivered at general conference in October 1998:

> Now, brethren, I want to make it very clear that I am not prophesying, that I am not predicting years of famine in the future. But I am suggesting that the time has come to get our houses in order.
>
> So many of our people are living on the very edge of their incomes. In fact, some are living on borrowings. . . .
>
> . . . I am troubled by the huge consumer installment debt which hangs over the people of the nation, including our own people. In March 1997 that debt totaled $1.2

trillion, which represented a 7 percent increase over the previous year. . . .

I recognize that it may be necessary to borrow to get a home, of course. But let us buy a home that we can afford and thus ease the payments which will constantly hang over our heads without mercy or respite for as long as 30 years. . . .

. . . What a wonderful feeling it is to be free of debt, to have a little money against a day of emergency put away where it can be retrieved when necessary.

President Faust would not tell you this himself. Perhaps I can tell it, and he can take it out on me afterward. He had a mortgage on his home drawing 4 percent interest. Many people would have told him he was foolish to pay off that mortgage when it carried so low a rate of interest. But the first opportunity he had to acquire some means, he and his wife determined they would pay off their mortgage. He has been free of debt since that day. That's why he wears a smile on his face, and that's why he *whistles while he works.*

I urge you, brethren, to look to the condition of your finances. I urge you to be modest in your expenditures; discipline yourselves in your purchases to avoid debt to the extent possible. *Pay off your debt as quickly as you can, and free yourselves from bondage.*[1]

Ten years later, almost to the day, global stock markets tumbled and sent us into economic turmoil. Like the prophets of old, a modern prophet had warned us. Did you notice the two debts our prophet was most concerned about? They were huge installment (or consumer or credit card) debt and the practice of buying homes we could not afford (mortgage debt). Both of these practices have led us to our present economic circumstances. Only the Lord knows the future, but we must pray for the wisdom that he will give us to help us manage our individual economic conditions.

# Let Virtue Garnish Your Thoughts

Personal purity and righteousness lead to personal revelation, guidance, and comfort from the Holy Ghost. These are the fruits of faith. Money is governed most prudently when it is governed with honesty and integrity. Perhaps that is why one of the governing rules of finance is that we pay an honest tithe and a generous fast offering. Honesty and integrity allow the Lord to whisper to our minds and hearts the knowledge we will need to survive our own individual storm—whether that storm be a small downpour or a whopping hurricane. Paying an honest tithe opens the windows of heaven so much that there will not be room enough to receive the blessings the Lord pours out (Malachi 3:10).

This book will provide you with suggestions, but they will remain only suggestions until the Lord affirms them for you. He will direct your personal affairs if you let virtue garnish your thoughts. Therefore, if you listen to the prophets and heed your own individual promptings, you will come out on top.

# Cultivate a Spirit of Charity

Living successfully on less requires cooperation—cooperation with friends and neighbors and, especially, cooperation with your family. The following charitable principles will help you to govern your finances.

*Keep your finances common, and decide together how to spend your money.* A popular financial scenario has swept through the younger generation. They keep "his" accounts and "her" accounts. He manages a specific list of household expenses, including the mortgage and the utilities; she manages the rest, such as the groceries and the car payment. Neither the husband nor the wife converses about financial affairs. In time the lines between expenses blur, squabbles begin, and the family environment becomes unstable. We have never encountered a family that successfully managed their finances under such an arrangement.

Husbands, wives, and even children must work together for their common good in the spirit of charity.

*Beware of the "blame game."* Whether you are overspent, over-drawn, or overwhelmed with a mountain of debt, it does no good to try to affix blame for your economic storm. Blame does not solve problems and is counterproductive. Determine instead where you are, where you want to go, and how best to achieve lasting solutions to your situation. There is always enough cul-pability to go around. Even if one partner in a marriage is more responsible, the other partner is still somewhat to blame.

*Don't use money as a weapon.* In twenty years of marriage Sally was never allowed to assist her husband in creating their budget. For five years, despite inflation, pay raises, and growing children, he gave her the same fixed amount of dollars to feed their fam-ily. The amount did not keep pace with their needs, yet Sally's husband refused to reconsider allowing her to spend more. Sally began to resent not just the miserly allowance but her husband as well. A family plan has to be a *family* plan.

*Teach your children about prudent spending.* Children need to have at least a minimal understanding of your family's con-straints. While they do not need to know every detail, they need to comprehend the costs of utilities, food, housing, and transpor-tation. Such knowledge will eventually prepare them for their own day of independence. When children understand costs, they not only cooperate but also become advocates of frugality. They learn the wisdom of saving for luxuries, and they become mindful of waste.

*Establish neighborhood co-ops.* Tools and garden equipment can be shared through a well-structured neighborhood co-op, which distributes the economic benefit of much-needed equipment. Shovels, rakes, garden tillers, lawnmowers, and other tools can be shared under a partnering arrangement that can be especially beneficial during turbulent times.

*Share promotions and bulk-food purchases.* Friends, neigh-bors, and extended family can share warehouse bulk purchases and memberships. Two-for-one promotions can also be shared, whether you are buying shoes or going out for dinner.

*Make friendships mutually beneficial.* Don't pass up an opportunity to make a friend, whether that friend is a clerk, a salesman, or a tradesman. Friends help friends. A friend who works in a store that carries something you hope to buy will keep you informed when the store is having a sale. A friend who works as a mechanic will cut you a special deal on your next automobile repair. A friend who sells used cars will tell you when just the right vehicle at the right price shows up on his lot. The most modest person you meet may be the very person who offers you a lifeline when you are drowning financially. In turn, be a friend yourself.

*Share coupons.* Coupons are a good way to save money, but some people have more coupons than they will ever use. Why not share surplus coupons with your friends, family, and neighbors? You might even make those exchanges fun times. Coupons could be exchanged during neighborhood potluck lunches or during other activities.

*Exchange goods and services.* Trying times can bring out the best in people, allowing them to more easily exchange, share, and barter goods and services. Neighbors can pool garden produce and share their surplus with the hungry. Children's hand-me-downs can be passed between friends. The gifted baker can trade pies, cakes, and bread for haircuts from a cosmetologist neighbor. Babysitting, music lessons, tutoring, gardening, and even automobile and household repairs can be exchanged with friends and family, as can clothing, books, music, DVDs, and games. Men can exchange sports equipment. Women can exchange personal services such as manicures, pedicures, and facials. Everyone benefits when friends and neighbors share. Create social opportunities that allow for the exchange of goods and services.

*Share spring cleanup.* In the springtime the men of your neighborhood can assist each other with yard cleanup, garden tilling, and air-conditioning preparation. After we moved into our neighborhood, all the neighbors turned out when someone was ready to plant seed or lay sod for their new lawn. This made the work fun.

## Organize and Prepare Yourself

*Keep good records.* We live such a fast-paced lifestyle that keeping good records seems too time consuming, but doing so will save considerable time and money over your lifetime. Whether recording your spending, balancing your budget, or organizing important papers, good records reap huge windfalls. Most of the time spent in organization comes at the beginning. Maintaining records from then on is actually easier than searching for important paperwork when it is critical.

Many books and Web sites offer document-organizing materials. A document-organizing system we have enjoyed was initially developed for senior citizens. We think you'll find it readily adaptable to individuals and families of any size. It is found at www .TodaysSeniors.com.

Precisely what documents should you keep? Tax statements and receipts relating to itemized deductions (donations, business expenses, and interest payments), warranties, retirement account statements, stubs from your utility and other similar monthly bills, insurance policies and addenda, and automobile and major appliance service manuals and warranties should all be carefully and conveniently filed. In addition, you might consider keeping the receipts of major purchases such as furniture, electronic equipment, appliances, automobiles, and mortgage papers. These receipts prove date of purchase.

Documentation of date of sale and warranty will save you money when replacement or repairs become necessary. Over the years we have saved hundreds of dollars by keeping the sales receipt and the warranty together in our filing cabinet for all our major purchases.

*Dispose of credit card debt.* Carrying a balance on a credit card is a bad idea because credit cards have become the biggest budget buster in the history of families. Despite slick advertising to the contrary, all credit cards do is whop you with interest on small purchases—as much as an 18–21 percent annual percentage rate (APR) for everything you keep on the cards until paid in full. The lunch you charged today could ultimately cost you dearly. Twenty years from now you might still be paying for it. We'll talk more about credit cards later, but for now just keep in mind that a part of organization and preparation is to get rid of unnecessary expenses. If every penny counts, why spend more than you have to?

Though plastic has become a way of life, nothing makes that giant sucking sound more than credit card payments and ballooning interest. Here is how it works: If you have a balance of $5,000 at 18 percent APR, it will take you twenty-six years to pay the balance in full if you make only the minimum payment. By the time you pay off the balance, you will have spent more than $12,000 for that original $5,000 debt. That's a loss of $7,000. What could you do with $7,000? Unfortunately, your loss won't end there.

Suppose you slip up and your payment arrives late? That eventually happens to all of us, and when it does, we face added fees and penalties. In addition, our interest rate may increase even more—maybe on several cards, not just on that one card. Credit card companies share late-payment information. In tough economic times, credit card companies hurt more than other businesses. They have to find a way to make up for their losses. The result? More fees and more ways of forcing us to pay them. We'll discuss this in length later. For now just remember: Don't use your credit card unless absolutely necessary, and always pay the balance in full at the end of every month.

*Keep your bills in an established and easily accessible place.* Scan through your bills frequently, paying attention to due dates. Never take a due date for granted because card companies, utilities, and other creditors can change the payment date without informing you in advance. Your statement is your only notice of the due date. Save yourself from paying finance charges and late fees. Each dollar you spend on a fee wastes your money.

In addition, before paying your bills, examine them for inaccuracies. Don't assume a statement is correct. Over the years we've heard it all—a clerical error that turned a $10 purchase into a $100,000 purchase, a shopping trip in Texas charged to a Utah cardholder who had never set foot in that state, a string of long-distance phone calls not even dialed from your number to a state halfway across the continent. It's not that your creditor is trying to be deceptive, but mistakes happen, computers malfunction, and the zero key on the keypad sometimes sticks. If you find that you have been erroneously charged for something, dispute the bill by phone and document the name of the person you speak with. If necessary, dispute the bill by letter as well. It is hard to argue with evidence in your favor. Keep after it and stay positive, even if you have to call and write several times before a dispute is resolved.

Also look over your bills on a regular basis for services *you can do without.* Make it a practice to call everyone who sends you a bill at least once a year to ask about ways in which you can save money. Service providers may suggest purchasing packages of service or tell you about a special promotion that will reduce the size of your bill.

*Save money against a rainy day.* We all receive expected and unexpected windfalls. Rebate checks, income tax refunds, birthday money, salary bonuses, and all or a portion of the two extra paychecks you receive each year if you are paid semiweekly can be put into your rainy-day savings account. It is a good idea to have cash for at least three months for emergencies and other unexpected expenses. For those who struggle from paycheck to paycheck, sudden costs can seem insurmountable. But a few dollars saved here and there can add up. Next time the car breaks down, the roof begins to leak, the furnace goes out, or you lose your job, your three months of savings should see you through.

*Use up everything, and return unused items.* We like to think we always stay on top of things, but we don't. We confess that we have a lot of half-used products and that we have purchased many products that we don't need, no longer desire, or neglected to take back. This is where good organization saves you time and money. Establish places where *stuff* can collect in a clean, organized fashion. Store your food according to an organized, easy-to-find system. Clean your refrigerator and your freezer, and place like items together so you can use up food before it expires or spoils.

If you buy in bulk you will undoubtedly have a number of products you will not be able to use. Exchange with friends or family members all of your extra napkins, paper plates, dry cereals, and similar products. Take back in a timely fashion anything you don't need, and get your money back.

Whenever you are involved in a household project or a special event, you will probably have unused products left over. If a package is unopened and your receipt is readily accessible, take it back rather than store it. You'll be surprised how much these purchases add up.

# Seek for Wisdom, Not Riches

*Be patient.* Patience is its own reward. At times we all buy things on impulse that a day or two later we regret buying. The impulse to buy can be expelled by a short walk away from the item or by holding it for thirty seconds to think it over. If it doesn't seem that important after a short wait, it isn't something we really need or want.

If you are thinking of making a major purchase, never buy without talking to your spouse first. Then both of you should sleep on it. Sales come and go, and good deals can be had any time. You'll seldom miss out too much by taking the time to think things through. Be wise.

*Compare prices on major purchases.* Comparing prices allows you additional time to think. Never make large purchases without an established budget and without doing some price and quality comparisons. We have watched ads and perused stores over extended periods—years sometimes—waiting for just the price we were willing to pay. We have never been sorry we waited.

*Don't buy the latest and greatest.* Markets fluctuate, and demand determines price. Being the last one on the block to purchase the newest technology is not foolish; it is absolutely sensible. Price inevitably drops dramatically on new technology after a year or two, and quality inevitably improves. You'll be sorry if you are the first to buy the newest and greatest gadget. Technology is a developing process, and you don't want to be the one stuck with a high-priced product riddled with bugs.

*Look at the small stuff.* "Folks can cut 20 to 30 percent of their expenses by looking at the small stuff," says Ric Edelman, author of *Ordinary People, Extraordinary Wealth.* "You don't need all those premium cable channels. . . . You need to recognize that you're throwing away money on things that have no long-term impact on your life."[2]

*Own what you can afford.* Always ask yourself, "Do I really need this?" Everyone wants a beautiful home, the newest car, and the latest fashion, but is the purchase worth sleepless nights riddled with worry? Your money is better saved for big dreams down the road such as your retirement or your children's education and missions.

*Don't walk into a store without a spending limit.* Shop the ads. If you walk into a store without an ad, look for one near the entrance. Many stores post their ads in the foyer. Buy when price is lowest, and buy only what you can afford.

*If something you bought goes on sale within a few weeks after your purchase, return it and ask for the sale price.* If you return it within ten days or a month, depending on a store's policy, you can ask for and receive a price adjustment. Always remember to bring in your receipt.

*Know how to spot a real discount.* Stores occasionally rid themselves of display merchandise and opened or returned items. These special clearances yield the biggest savings. Sometimes you can buy new or nearly new products for a fraction of their original price. Find out when your favorite retailers will have their special clearance sales. These sales are especially good when it comes to clothing or furniture. Some companies even refurbish defective products and resell them at deep discounts—sometimes with the original warranty. Special sales are generally final, so look over your merchandise and try it out, searching for defects, before you commit.

A friend of ours was in the market for a tool chest. He knew what he wanted, but he didn't feel he could afford the high price. He went to a major retailer and asked if there were any returned tool chests. "I have five returned chests," a clerk said. "Come with me and I'll show them to you."

Some were slightly scratched, some were dented, and one sported a half-off price tag because it lacked wheels.

"I'll take the one without the wheels," our friend told the clerk. He knew he could find wheels at a hardware store and put them on himself. Imagine our friend's surprise, however, when he later found the missing wheels taped to the bottom of one of the drawers.

*Look for house brands.* House brands are not limited to food. House brands cover a wide variety of products. They are generally identical in quality to name brands; they lack only the slicker packaging and marketing.

*Contract in the off-season.* Contractors and home repairs are generally less costly in the off-season. New cars, RVs, appliances, and electronic equipment are sold at their lowest price just prior to the new model year. If you don't know a product's "season," ask a clerk.

# Conclusion

Living by faith, being obedient to the Lord, extending charity, organizing, and avoiding impulses are the secrets to living on less. In addition, never allow yourself to become discouraged. The abundant life is never achieved in a straight course. Unforeseen obstacles can and will present themselves. Financial storms come and go whether they are personal or global. Just stay the course.

Frugal living may not pay big dividends initially, but over time you'll find you no longer need to live paycheck to paycheck. Judge yourself not on how far you have yet to go but on how far you've come. Success, like money, comes a little at a time.

# Chapter 2

# Putting a Price Tag on Happiness

"I am come," said Jesus, "that they might have life, and that they might have it more abundantly" (John 10:10). What makes for the happy, fulfilling, abundant life of which the Savior spoke? Evidently a lot of people think that a happy life begins with money. From October 5 to November 6, 2005, the Pew Research Center asked 3,014 people whether they were happy. Just more than a third (34 percent) responded that they were happy. Another half said they were pretty happy, and 15 percent claimed they were not happy at all.

We have often heard that money cannot buy happiness, but Pew's respondents appear to contradict that aphorism. While only 24 percent who made under $30,000 a year said they were happy, 49 percent of those who made $100,000 or more said they were happy. Is the aphorism wrong?

Key social indicators also contradict the Pew finding. From 1960 to the turn of the new century, the divorce rate doubled, the teen suicide rate tripled, violent crime quadrupled, the percent of babies born to unmarried parents increased six-fold, cohabitation increased sevenfold, and the rate of depression soared ten times higher than the pre-World War II level.[1]

In 2003 a World Value Survey of people in sixty-five nations, published in the British magazine *New Scientist,* found that the world's happiest people live in Nigeria, Mexico, Venezuela, El Salvador, and Puerto Rico—hardly the most affluent countries on the planet. This same survey described the desire for material goods as a "happiness suppressant."[2]

In July 2004, Richard Ernsberger wrote in an article in *Newsweek International:*

> We Americans are told in our Declaration of Independence that three things are sacrosanct—"life, liberty, and the pursuit of happiness." And like fellow hedonists in Asia, Europe and elsewhere, we've clearly taken the message to heart. We work hard, earn lots of money and spend gleefully on iPods, flat-screen TVs, SUVs and all sorts of expensive fripperies. We indulge, we gratify—and therefore we *expect* to be the happiest . . . people on the planet. So why aren't we?[3]

David G. Myers, social psychologist at Hope College, bemoaned the decline of our society. He referred to it as "life, liberty, and the *purchase* of happiness."[4] In 1958, John Kenneth Galbraith described the United States as "the affluent society" in his book by the same name. If 1958 America was an affluent society, today is doubly affluent.

"Americans today own twice as many cars, eat out twice as often, enjoy big screen color TVs, microwave ovens, home computers, air conditioning, Post-it notes, and gobs of goodies."[5] On the other hand, according to another study, since 1957 the number of Americans who describe themselves as happy has actually declined from 35 to 30 percent.[6]

No one has experienced the highs and lows of affluence more vividly than lottery winners. Most have gone from near poverty to millionaires in a matter of minutes. Matthew Herper of *Forbes* magazine reported that "surveys have found virtually the same level of happiness between the very rich individuals on the Forbes 400 and the Maasai herdsmen of East Africa." Lottery winners may experience an initial rush they might translate as happiness, but it does not translate into long-term contentment. These same surveys discovered that lotto winners returned to their previous level of happiness after five years.[7]

Evelyn Adams, who won the New Jersey lottery not just once but twice (in 1985 and again in 1986) and collected $5.4 million, now lives in a trailer. Her money is gone. "Everybody wanted my money," she said. "Everybody had their hand out. I never learned one simple word in the English language—'No.' I wish I had the chance to do it all over again. I'd be much smarter about it now." When given an opportunity to do something like it another time, she wasn't any wiser. She lost money on slot machines in Atlantic City.

She was not alone. Ask Suzanne Mullins. Ms. Mullins won the Virginia lottery in 1993 and collected a whopping $4.2 million. Her dream came to an abrupt end, however. Using her windfall as collateral, she borrowed money; soon she was deeply in debt—her money was gone. Or ask Ken Proxmire who won $1 million in the Michigan lottery. He used his winnings to open a California car business with his brothers, only to close the doors in bankruptcy five short years later and return to his original job as a machinist. Saddest of all is the case of Willie Hurt of Lansing, Michigan. The day he won $3.1 million in 1989 must have seemed like the greatest day in his life, but two years later he lost his wife through a costly divorce, suffered from crack cocaine addiction, and faced murder charges. He was broken, alone, and penniless. Unfortunately, these stories are more typical than they are anecdotal.[8]

David G. Myers summed it up: "I have called this soaring wealth and shrinking spirit 'the American paradox.' More than ever, we at the end of the last century were finding ourselves with big houses and broken homes, high incomes and low morale, secured rights and diminished civility. We were excelling at making a living but too often failing to make a life. We celebrated our prosperity but yearned for purpose. We cherished our freedoms but longed for connection. In an age of plenty, we were feeling spiritual hunger."[9]

So if money doesn't buy happiness, what does? Professor Ed Diener of the University of Illinois tells us that satisfaction is achieved most often through social relationships. People who score high on life have close and supportive family and friends. Other positive influences include work, school, or performance in an important role such as being a homemaker or a grandparent. Working toward goals brings self-satisfaction, and satisfaction coupled with learning and growth contribute to an abundant life.[10]

Myers adds his own list of ingredients to achieving the good life: close and supportive relationships, intimate friendships or a committed marriage, connection to a faith community, optimism, self-esteem, the perception that one is in control of life, and work and leisure experiences that engage one's skills.[11]

After spending years in his laboratory studying the nature of human happiness, Harvard professor Daniel Gilbert published *Stumbling on Happiness,* a best seller and winner of the 2007 Royal Society Prize for Science Books. Gilbert knows something personal about happiness. Within a short time his mentor passed away, his mother died, his marriage fell apart, and his teenage son developed problems at school. As bad as his situation was, he picked himself up and went on with his life. One day at lunch he told a friend going though his own difficult times, "If you'd have asked me a year ago how I'd deal with all this, I'd have predicted that I couldn't get out of bed in the morning." It was that remark that sparked his research.

The truth, as Professor Gilbert discovered, is that bad things don't affect us as profoundly as we expect them to. He found that the same is true of good things. "As a species, we tend to be moderately happy with whatever we get. If you take a scale that goes from zero to 100, people, generally, report their happiness at about 75. We keep trying to get to 100. Sometimes we get there. But we don't stay long.

"We certainly fear the things that would get us down to 20 or 10—the death of a loved one, the end of a relationship, a serious challenge to our health. But when those things happen, most of us will return to our emotional baselines more quickly than we'd predict. Humans are wildly resilient."[12]

As we researched this chapter, we discovered a long-forgotten high school essay written by one of our sons. He wrote: "Money can cause some problems with your life management. Sometimes people need to manage their life and use it to bring happiness. . . . Money brings only temporary joy, but you need some to be happy. . . . Once someone has obtained affluence they begin to look for more in their life. They begin to look for something that puts a purpose back into life and gives them a fulfilled feeling."

The scriptures provide us with the seeds of happiness: Bring souls to Christ, help the poor, keep the commandments, pray and have faith, demonstrate the pure love of Christ (charity), serve with all your heart, forgive others, and develop humility. Once we discover that happiness does not come with a price tag, we are on the path to living a full life at half the price.

# Chapter 3

# Do I Really Need This?

On July 7, 2005, Alex Martin, a Seattle-area choreographer, undertook an unusual experiment. She made herself a simple brown dress and decided she would wear it every day for an entire year. She washed her dress every two or three days, mended it often, and replaced the buttons many times. In the winter she adorned her dress with two sweaters she'd purchased through Goodwill. Whenever the temperature allowed, she wore the dress solo.

What did people think? At first most of the people in her professional circle never noticed that she wore the same dress every day. That surprised her. She thought people took note of what she wore, but she discovered that most people were so consumed with their *own* appearance that they didn't notice or care about hers. She also discovered that when people learned about her experiment, they almost universally loved it. They wished they had the courage to do the same.

She kept a blog and allowed others to write their comments, which included the following:

"Hi, I read about your project. . . . I just wanted to let you know I felt the same way. I think it is a very novel idea. I haven't had time to read your journal yet, but I think Americans need to reduce the emphasis and obsession on possessions. We are so consumed with owning and having."

"Congratulations on wearing your 'little brown dress' for 365 days. You are an inspiration. I have a son and stepson in their last semesters of college starting tomorrow. Luckily both my husband and I are VERY frugal. However, as this last semester approaches, I am even MORE frugal, and you are inspiring me to NOT SPEND ONE PENNY other than what I have through all of 2007. . . . I already pretty much DO this, but you are helping me to do it even with a greater vengeance!"

When Martin was asked how this experience changed her, she replied: "That answer is huge and long. . . . I know that I'm even more engaged and interested in this whole line of thinking than I was when I started the project. I don't know whether to call it the 'intentional wardrobe' or a 'fashion de-tox diet' or a 'slow clothing movement,' but I am swimming deep in this topic and not even considering a return to a normal wardrobe at this point."[1]

By the way, for the entire year Martin spent less than $20 on her personal wardrobe.

Judith Levine, an author from Vermont, launched a similar experiment. She went a year without buying any extras and chronicled her adventures in a book titled *Not Buying It: My Year Without Shopping*. For 365 days Levine and a friend bought only essentials. She never saw a movie, went to the theater, dined out, or bought ice cream or a cup of coffee.

"We got pretty good at finding free things to do," she said. "We would take walks, go to the park, find free concerts and free festivals."

Other friends were intrigued by the experiment. Most wanted to curb their own spending as well, but they couldn't control their spending and gave up. One day one friend moaned in exasperation, "Oh, Judith, not another walk!"

The best part of Levine's experiment was not just that she paid off her $8,000 credit card debt but that she gained so much in personal relationships. "One thing about not buying stuff is that you end up with a lot of time. Once you have more hours on your hands, you can give more time to people. . . . You not only learn what you can live without but what you really want to spend your money on."[2]

Many of us have lived an affluent life for nearly a lifetime. Our abundance has made us so we can no longer distinguish the difference between essential and nonessential. We want an iPod. We yearn for it. Thoughts about that wonderful iPod consume our life for several days. We simply must buy one—today! So out we go and buy the first iPod we see. It satisfies us for about a week, and then we put it aside. Our yearnings change. We almost need to want something else. Maybe it is a new refrigerator, a new car, or a new home. The cycle goes on and on.

# Essential vs. Nonessential

The purpose of this chapter is to acquaint you with principles that will allow you and your family to make the distinction between the essential and the nonessential. Do not expect that just one reading will make you an expert. It will take a lifetime of trial and error to perfect the elimination of the nonessential. Taken in its entirety, this book is meant to assist you in finding that "comfortable place" where you and your family feel "in control" of your money. There is no concrete right and wrong when it comes to identifying your family's needs and wants. Every family is unique. Every family lives its own lifestyle. Hence, you must include the Lord in making decisions that will be most beneficial to you. Only the Lord, in his omnipotence, knows you and knows your needs. What is a need to one family may be a want to another. Find your own "comfortable place."

In the following sections, you will find a wide variety of tips and suggestions for saving money. These may seem at first blush to be no more than long lists. We invite you to look past the lists and to discover the resource they might be to your family. We have included many cost-saving methods that many families have employed successfully for years. These methods have allowed them to trim the fat from their budget. Some may seem obvious to you, but others may become the key to your success. How you spend your money should be a family decision. Otherwise, expenditures will become a source of contention and hard feelings. Read through the tips and suggestions and discuss them with your family.

To be successful, *do not* try to make too many changes all at once; you will only get discouraged if you do. Implement small changes at first and work up to larger lifestyle changes. Don't make this process overwhelming. Take time to evaluate your money-saving measures with your family and really listen to their input. A little change here and a little change there will ease you into a new lifestyle. For those who need to make drastic cuts because of a job loss, financial setback, or rising mound of debt, the changes will have to be more drastic.

Never assume that you are doing everything completely right and that there is nothing you can learn. We can all learn something, and we can all adapt to changing circumstances. Economic downturns are always beneficial because they allow us the opportunity to reevaluate and simplify our lives.

You might begin by holding a family council. Sit down with your spouse and your children who are old enough to understand. Bring the necessary paperwork so you can look over the previous month's expenditures. You can use a check register, a bank statement, or a computer printout. Next to each expenditure, write E for essential or NE nonessential. (Perhaps you'll prefer N for need and W for want.) Then separate the essentials from the nonessentials and make new lists. You may even want to total the costs associated with the Essential list and compare them to the total costs of the Nonessential list. This will allow you to consider the expenses you might trim from your family budget. Have you trimmed enough? If not, go back and move even more items from the Essential list to the Nonessential list.

Even subcategories contain nonessential expenses. For

example, a purchase at a grocery store will undoubtedly include many nonessential items. The same may be true for automobile expenses, insurance, and even utilities (is cable TV part of your utility bill?). Nonessentials can be found in every category of your budget. We'll help you spot these with the money-saving tips in the next section.

If you even halved the total of your nonessential expenses, how much money could you save? Are you beginning to see light at the end of the tunnel? You should. Completing this one exercise will put you on the path to living a full life without feeling much of a pinch.

We know a couple who took this exercise a step further. They kept a notebook with them for an entire month. Each time they bought something, they wrote it down. Each week they took five or ten minutes to look over the notebook. It gave them a better grasp on their spending. More important, by writing everything down they found that they didn't make many impulse purchases.

## Be Patient

We have already told you how crucial it is to be patient. Make it your practice to hold an item in your hands at least ten seconds before you place it in your cart and ask, "Do I really need this?" The more an item costs, the longer you should take to answer the question. For example, if you intend to buy a car or an appliance, try waiting thirty days. Then, if you still want the item, it's probably essential. After thirty days the impulse to purchase nonessential items will usually pass.

## Determine the Real Cost

Think in terms of real cost versus the cost per month before making your decisions. It may cost you $50 a month for cable TV. You can surely afford $50 a month, but in a year that adds up to $600. Is it worth $600?

You see a car you like. The salesman tells you it is a steal—just $287 a month. The car is priced at $15,000, and you will make sixty payments to pay it off. That means you will actually pay $17,220 for it—an extra $2,220.

# Look for Less-expensive Alternatives

If you spend even $15 a month to rent DVDs, in a year you'll spend $180. But if you prefer to rent DVDs rather than spend more for cable or satellite, rent the DVDs and drop the cable or satellite. Add up all the CDs, newspapers, magazines, and books you buy, and then look at alternatives. Can you borrow from the library or from friends? Can you find the same material on the Internet?

Your dinner and night at the movies with friends might be as costly as your groceries for a week. Friends might be just as happy to spend time alone with you in your home playing a game or talking and eating popcorn.

A current and popular belief is that it costs less for a cell phone than for a landline. But does it really? Research shows that the situation fluctuates. The safer assumption is to research and evaluate your telephone options frequently, compare prices between cell phones and landlines and compare the contract price between cell suppliers. Telecommunications is a cutting-edge business and each year new options open for the savvy consumer. There are attractive, introductory bundles of landline telephone, cable or satellite television, and Internet. There are computer-to-computer calling options. Every year brings new technology and new choices for cost-savings. Keep current and up-to-date. Look for not only savings but for quality service.

Whatever option you decide upon, however, will require a periodic review. Let's use your cell phone as an example. How recently have you reviewed your statement? Are you paying for extras you use infrequently or never at all like text messaging, pictures, or e-mail? Can you do without any of these extras? Can you really afford them? Don't be afraid to make changes, even sacrifices when the situation warrants. You can return to your comfortable frills when you can afford them.

What about your long-distance service? Have you compared prices recently to see if you are still receiving the lowest price possible? What about phone service through the Internet? How costly is that, and how well does the service work in your area? Find out by doing some research on the Internet.

# Free Services over the Internet

We have discovered a fabulous Web site to calculate savings. It is called "Feed the Pig" and is found at www.feedthepig.org. A few minutes on this site will prove invaluable to you and your family. Visit it and identify where your family might be spending more than is needed.

The Internet is also a vast resource for free budgeting services—everything from open office to household budget spreadsheets. Here is a sampling of household spreadsheets that can be downloaded from www.christianpf.com/10-free-household-budget -spreadsheets.

- Household budget template—allows you to input each purchase and compare your total amount spent to the amount budgeted.

- Personal budget monthly spreadsheet—good for adding up income and expenses and finding out the difference between the two.

- Family budget planner—allows you to look at a whole year's expenses and income month by month.

- Wedding budget template—provides suggestions on how much you should spend on each wedding item.

- Budget spreadsheets—allow you to look at your budget by pay period instead of by month.

- Debt-reduction spreadsheet—shows you a snowball method for reducing your debt. The first sheet is a basic calculator, and the second gives you a printable payment schedule.

- Personal budget worksheet—a simple but proven way to add up your expenses and your income and see the difference.

- Detailed personal budgeting Excel sheet—thorough step-by-step spreadsheet to guide you through the budgeting process.[3]

Of course, we provide many of these same spreadsheets and more in our first book, *Debt-Free on Any Income.* You can decide which option works best for your budget.

In conclusion, keeping the question, "Do I really need this?" uppermost in your mind shields you from mounds of unwanted and unneeded expense. It is only a simple question, but it has enormous consequences. Remember the days when there were no cell phones or iPods or big-screen TVs? Has your grandmother told you about the days the family sat on the steps in the cool of the evening because they had no air conditioning? Did you play games with the neighborhood kids at twilight on a summer's eve? Did you ever lie on the cool green grass and look up at the sky? Simplify your life and regain control of it.

# PART TWO

# Spend Less and Be Happy

# Chapter 4

# Family Fun on a Shoestring

We'll begin this section by viewing an avenue of household expense that we cannot afford to neglect without risking a sense of overall contentment. It is that contentment that allows us to feel we are living a full life. We speak of family fun. When Mary Poppins sang "A spoonful of sugar helps the medicine go down," she hit on a key element of family order. Even during family difficulties, you still cannot neglect that which brings joy to your life. To be successful in implementing change, begin with a spoonful of sugar.

"String!" shouted Brother, bursting into the kitchen. "We need lots more string."

It was Saturday. As always, it was a busy one, for "Six days shalt thou labor and do all thy work" was taken seriously then. Outside, Father and Mr. Patrick next door were doing chores.

Inside the two houses, Mother and Mrs. Patrick were engaged in spring cleaning. Such a windy March day was ideal for "turning out" clothes closets. Already woolens flapped on backyard clotheslines.

Somehow the boys had slipped away to the back lot with kites. Now, even at the risk of having Brother impounded to beat carpets, they had sent him for more string. Apparently there was no limit to the heights to which kites would soar today.

My mother looked out the window. The sky was piercingly blue; the breeze fresh and exciting. Up in all that blueness sailed great puffy billows of clouds. It had been a long, hard winter, but today was spring.

Mother looked at the sitting room, its furniture disordered for a Spartan sweeping. Again her eyes wavered toward the window. "Come on, girls! Let's take string to the boys and watch them fly the kites a minute."

On the way we met Mrs. Patrick, laughing guiltily, escorted by her girls.

There never was such a day for flying kites! God doesn't make two such days in a century. We played all our fresh twine into the boys' kites and still they soared. We could hardly distinguish the tiny, orange-colored specks. Now and then we slowly reeled one in, finally bringing it dipping and tugging to earth, for the sheer joy of sending it up again. What a thrill to run with them, to the right, to the left, and see our poor, earthbound movements, reflected minutes later in the majestic sky-dance of the kites! We wrote wishes on slips of paper and slipped them over the string. Slowly, irresistibly, they climbed up until they reached the kites. Surely, all such wishes would be granted!

Even our fathers dropped hoe and hammer and joined us. Our mothers took their turn, laughing like schoolgirls. Their hair blew out of their pompadours and curled loose about their cheeks; their gingham aprons whipped about their legs. Mingled with our fun was something akin to awe. The grownups were really playing with us! Once I looked at Mother and thought she looked actually pretty. And her over forty!

We never knew where the hours went on that hilltop

that day. There were no hours, just a golden, breezy Now. I think we were all a little beyond ourselves. Parents forgot their duty and their dignity; children forgot their combativeness and small spites. "Perhaps it's like this in the kingdom of heaven," I thought confusedly.

It was growing dark before, drunk with sun and air, we all stumbled sleepily back to the houses. I suppose there must have been a surface tidying-up, for the house on Sunday looked decorous enough.

The strange thing was, we didn't mention that day afterward. I felt a little embarrassed. Surely none of the others had thrilled to it as deeply as I. I locked the memory up in that deepest part of me where we keep "the things that cannot be and yet are."

The years went on, then one day I was scurrying about my own kitchen in a city apartment, trying to get some work out of the way while my three-year-old insistently cried her desire to "go park and see ducks."

"I can't go!" I said. "I have this and this to do, and when I'm through I'll be too tired to walk that far."

My mother, who was visiting us, looked up from the peas she was shelling. "It's a wonderful day," she offered; "really warm, yet there's a fine, fresh breeze. It reminds me of the day we flew the kites."

I stopped in my dash between stove and sink. The locked door flew open, and with it a gush of memories. I pulled off my apron. "Come on," I told my little girl. "You're right, it's too good a day to miss."

Another decade passed. We were in the aftermath of a great war. All evening we had been asking our returned soldier, the youngest Patrick boy, about his experiences as a prisoner of war. He had talked freely, but now for a long time he had been silent. What was he thinking of—what dark and dreadful things?

"Say!" A smile twitched his lips. "Do you remember

. . . no, of course you wouldn't. It probably didn't make the impression on you it did on me."

I hardly dared speak. "Remember what?"

"I used to think of that day a lot in PW camp, when things weren't too good. Do you remember the day we flew the kites?"

Winter came, and the sad duty of a call of condolence on Mrs. Patrick, recently widowed. I dreaded the call. I couldn't imagine how Mrs. Patrick would face life alone.

We talked a little of my family and her grandchildren and the changes in the town. Then she was silent, looking down at her lap. I cleared my throat. Now I must say something about her loss, and she would begin to cry.

When she looked up, Mrs. Patrick was smiling. "I was sitting here thinking," she said. "Henry had such fun that day. Frances, do you remember the day we flew the kites?"[1]

It isn't the great big costly days that children and parents cherish years after they have passed; it is those little days, those days when we do something small but significant, those days we make a memory.

In that spirit, let's discuss some ideas for having fun with your family—ideas that cost little but might well create significant impact.

# Frugal Family Home Evenings and Fun Nights

Trips to Disneyland and expensive amusement parks might be fun but perhaps not nearly as memorable as scaled-back versions. Things you can do any day and any week of the year with simple planning and little money can be just as memorable. Consider placing ideas for family fun into a jar and periodically drawing them out and implementing them for your enjoyment.

*Street games.* Take a walk down memory lane and teach your children the games that delighted you as a child: kick the can, hula hoop, Red Rover, dodgeball, tag, and Mother, May I? If you can't remember too many games, there are sites online for games and game rules to jog your memory. In addition, many wonderful books with game suggestions are available at the library.

*Board games.* There is no end to the fun board games your family can play, including Scrabble, hangman, concentration, Monopoly, Battleship, Pictionary, Charades, and Trivial Pursuit. Search through your boxes and closets, dust off a few, and try them tonight. Go to your parents' or grandparents' homes and see what board games they may still have around. If you can't find any, visit a thrift store or check the Internet for used games. If you decide to buy a few, look for games without bells and whistles. These are generally the most fun and last the longest because they don't need repairs.

If your family enjoys playing electronic games together, don't be a sucker for a new title. Be patient. It may be only a matter of weeks before you can buy it at a discount. Or wait and buy it used. Many stores specialize in used electronic games. Rent games or purchase a game plan online or from a local store, but do so only if it is affordable.

Swap games with friends and neighbors, and ensure that you return them in as good a condition as when you borrowed them. You can also swap games or buy used games online.

Games can be both fun and educational. Your children can glean spelling, math, memory skills, and trivial knowledge from just a few moments playing games together.

*Nights without power.* When our children were young, they loved the nights the power went out. We'd grab a camping lantern or a candle or two and gather around the kitchen table or in the family room on pillows. On these nights Dad would read to us from a book of short stories, or sometimes we'd get out the snacks and play some of the board games we just mentioned. If your family needs some time together, turn off the lights, stop using the stove, and pretend it is a night without power.

*Craft night.* A craft night is a great opportunity for making model airplanes or cars and learning how to cross-stitch, crochet, knit, or quilt. Your family may enjoy making scrapbooks. Even Dad and the boys can have fun organizing and arranging family memories into delightful books. Children can be taught to sew on buttons or hem pants. Craft nights are fun, inexpensive, and educational.

*Movie night.* Why go out to watch a movie when you can do the same thing at home? Turn the lights down low, hook up a stereo to your entertainment system, and watch your favorite movie. We like classical movies you can check out from the library or used ones you can purchase online for pennies. Low-cost DVD rental services can fit almost any family's budget. Be sure to allow every member of the family a turn at making movie selections, and don't forget the popcorn and candy.

*Family party night.* You might have a family luau in the backyard complete with tiki torches, paper leis from the dollar store, and sale-priced pineapple with pulled-pork sandwiches. Another night your family could gather for a barbecue. In the summertime we hold old-fashioned ice cream socials complete with homemade ice cream and tons of fresh fruit, hot fudge, caramel sauce, and fresh berries. Or how about a night of homemade root beer and sparklers?

Family parties have become a tradition in our house. We go all out, but we try not to spend much money. We hold Christmas Eve parties with homemade foot-long sandwiches and chips and dip. We hold New Year's Eve parties with ice cream and shrimp. Our Fourth of July parties include slow-cooked beans, grilled hamburgers, and fireworks. Halloween is doughnut night. In addition, we have special pie nights, spaghetti nights, chili nights, taco nights, and homemade pizza nights.

*Backyard campout.* When going to the campground is out of the question or too expensive, set up a campout in the backyard.

Put up some tents, roll out the sleeping bags, play games, tell stories, and sing campfire songs. A blog we visited relates one family's tale of a campout in the family room in the dead of winter.

*Camping.* Don't neglect the real thing. Some of the finest moments we have spent were alone and away in a wilderness setting beside a roaring campfire. These are the moments when children and parents have only each other and can share secrets and express tender feelings. Take the time to spend time alone with your children.

*Picnics.* When the weather is nice, use any excuse for a picnic. Picnics can be at the neighborhood park, in the backyard, or on a blanket in your family room. If it's getting late, candles and camping lanterns can make your picnic more romantic. The food doesn't have to be fancy—even peanut butter, grilled cheese, or tuna fish will do. Just have fun!

*Raking leaves.* Make family work fun. Rake the leaves and before putting them in garbage sacks, let the children play in them a bit. Spring-cleaning might be backbreaking, but always end it with a family activity or treat to make it fun. Mix work with pleasure and you'll feel doubly satisfied.

*Museums and zoos.* Museums and zoos are fun and generally less expensive than other entertainment. Some public libraries offer discount passes to local museums. Also check your bank or credit union, as well as online, for discounts or passes. Take a large group of family and friends for even bigger discounts. If your family has a favorite zoo or museum and you live only a short distance away, consider a yearly membership.

# Hobbies

*Reading.* Reading is one of the least expensive and most beneficial hobbies in the world. Books are as close as the nearest public library. Also, used books can be purchased online or swapped with family, neighbors, and friends. Discuss the books you read with your family.

*Puzzles.* Whether you like Sudoku, crossword, or jigsaw puzzles, puzzles are fun, especially if you involve the whole family.

*Sports.* Take advantage of public facilities and community recreation centers. Many communities offer free tennis courts and basketball courts as well as low-cost swimming pools.

If you feel you must have a gym membership, shop around and find one you can both afford and dispose of quickly in the event of a family financial emergency.

Participate in sports that don't require expensive gear. If you need gear, buy it used. Check the ads in the newspaper and online, and shop garage sales.

Organize neighborhood sports groups for bicycling, rafting, running, and so forth. Look for groups that sponsor sports activities and competition.

*Community education.* School districts offer adult and family education classes. Take advantage of these. They teach skills as well as academic subjects.

*Collections.* Collecting things can be fun and interesting, particularly if the thing you collect is affordable. We've seen all kinds of collections—rocks, spoons, salt and pepper shakers, books, even barbed wire. The world is big and, with imagination, you can find many things to collect. Make sure you have the space, energy, and money to devote to your collection.

*Gardening.* Families can have loads of fun together growing flowers, shrubs, or vegetables. The benefits of gardening are enormous. Gardens provide a place to relax and are a great source of inexpensive food for the family table.

# Toys

Cheap is not always best. Buy quality toys that children will use and wear out. Always check for durability and safety. Some of our children's toys are now favorites of our grandchildren. Avoid toys with detachable pieces that can be lost or swallowed, and limit the number of battery-operated toys you buy. Batteries are expensive.

Look for toys that are educational and that encourage creativity. Our children loved blocks and Legos, construction sets, dolls, art supplies, science kits, nature kits, and children's crafts. If your children have more fun three days after Christmas with the boxes than with their new toys, you might consider buying fewer toys.

# Movie Theaters

Wait until a movie has been out for a few weeks and take advantage of discounts. Make it a practice to frequent matinees. Better yet, wait a month or two, and watch the movie at a discount movie theater. Check credit unions and banks for discounted theater tickets, or find them online.

# Family Vacations

Family vacations can be as exotic as a cruise or as simple as a trip to Grandma's, but if you follow a few rules you won't be paying for your vacation for years to come.

*Plan.* Make a plan and don't do it alone. Include everyone. Where do you want to go? How long will it take? How much money can you spend? It's never too early to begin planning a family vacation. Starting to plan in the middle of the winter when snow covers the ground is a great way to beat the winter doldrums. The more you plan and dream with your family, the greater the anticipation you will generate.

*Budget.* Make a spending plan. Budget for transportation, lodging, food, and activities, and then, just to be sure, add an additional 10 percent because whatever your plan, your vacation will cost more. Unexpected costs always arise despite the best plans, so be prepared financially. The key to success is to know in advance how much money you have to spend and to stick to your plan as closely as possible.

*Look for deals.* Do you need airfare, lodging, entertainment passes? Are you part of an organization that provides discounts—corporate, military, AAA, AARP? Compare online prices, make phone calls to find the best deals, and book things like airfare yourself to save an agent's fee. Consider taking your vacation in the off-season for greater savings. Look for a vacation package, and then add up costs to be sure that the package actually saves you money. Some package deals are not true discounts.

Inquire about bed-and-breakfast establishments. Consider camping for your lodging. Compare in advance the costs of various motels. Hotels.com contains a database of 85,000 properties and has a price-match guarantee of as much as 10–20 percent. Get advice from 20 million fellow travelers at tripadvisor.com.

If you must fly, consider traveling during the week rather than on weekends. Remember to factor in the cost of checked baggage. Some airlines charge one amount for the first checked bag and a higher amount for the second checked bag. Other airlines charge only for the second checked bag, so make sure you understand the airline's policy before you purchase a ticket. Most airlines state their baggage policy on their Web site. Keep in mind, however, that the cost of checked baggage applies to both the departure and return legs of your trip. Often this cost can make a significant difference in calculating the true cost of an airline ticket.

In addition, some airlines require that customers print out their own tickets before arriving at the airport. There may be a charge to have the airline print your ticket for you.

When booking travel, check a variety of sites for the best deal. Internet travel search engines are fabulous ways to find the best prices and many also allow you to book lodging and car rentals. These include priceline.com, expedia.com, orbitz.com, cheapflights .com, and kayak.com. Kayak.com searches hundreds of travel sites from all over the world, even smaller databases. It flags red-eye flights, long layovers, and short connection times to make your travel experience less stressful. Kayak.com does not book reservations; rather, once you click on a particular fare, you will be directed to the airline that provides that price. In addition, since flexibility provides the best opportunity for even lower rates, take advantage of Kayak.com's flexibility button to find the best price possible.

If you have waited until the last minute to book your flight, do not despair. You can visit www.lastminutedeals.com to find the lowest rates. Click on "last-second deals" for packages on flights, hotels, and car rentals.

Consider standby if it is available. If not, volunteer at the gate to give up your seat if the flight is overbooked. If you get bumped, the airline will probably offer you another ticket free in addition to your trip and maybe even a hotel for the night. Don't forget to use your frequent-flier miles.

When booking a rental car, pass up airport rental and go to a location just outside the airport or near to your hotel. These rental agencies will offer lower prices.

*Negotiate, haggle, and barter.* You aren't obligated to accept the price you are initially quoted. Motel owners get nothing for an empty room and may be happy to offer a discount, especially during the off-season. So ask for a discount. The worst they can say is no.

*Borrow or rent.* Consider borrowing or renting sports equipment, tents, backpacks, and especially big things like RVs, boats, Jet Skis, and four-wheelers.

*Prepare.* Check the weather forecast, bring proper clothing, and have maps, traveler's checks, an umbrella, sunblock, a first-aid kit, and emergency items for a hasty automobile repair such as jumper cables, belts, canned air for fixing flat tires, and so forth.

Eating on the road can be less expensive if you include a cooler packed with drinks, sandwich fixings, fruit, chips, and other things to munch on. Try making your own breakfast and lunch, and eat out just once a day to save on food.

# Chapter 5

# How to Avoid Starving to Death on Food

No facet of your household spending is more flexible than your food budget. There are basically four ways to cut food expenditures:

1. Eliminate waste.
2. Shop the sales.
3. Plan your meals and make a list.
4. Know how to shop.

## Eliminate Waste

The amount of food wasted on this planet is shocking. Timothy Jones, an anthropologist at the University of Arizona, discovered through his research that 40–50 percent of food ready for harvest *never gets eaten.* He found that there is enough edible food discarded to feed a good proportion of the starving people of the world and that if this situation were even partially corrected, U.S. consumers and manufacturers could save tens of billions of dollars each year as well as have less impact on the environment.[1]

Did you know that if just 5 percent of America's leftovers were recovered, they could feed four million people for one day? According to www.foodproductiondaily.com, "the U.N. World

Food Programme offers another way of looking at it: It says the total surplus of the U.S. alone could satisfy 'every empty stomach' in Africa (France's leftovers could feed the Democratic Republic of Congo; and Italy's could feed Ethiopia's undernourished)."[2] Did you know that disposing of food waste costs the U.S. $1 billion a year? Did you realize that rotting food releases a more potent methane, 20 times more damaging to the environment than carbon dioxide?[3]

The average American family of four tosses out 1.3 pounds of food every day, or 474.5 pounds per year. Household food waste computes to $43 billion annually and creates a serious economic problem.[4] When you add food waste from uneaten portions of meals and trimmings from food preparation at restaurants and cafeterias, the problem is even larger. The first step toward saving money on food, therefore, is to cut waste.

*Become more familiar with what is in your fridge and freezer.* Before finalizing your weekly grocery list, go to your refrigerator, freezer, and pantry. Do you know the expiration dates of everything you have? Use things up before they spoil or go stale. Particularly check dates on meats, fish, and prepared meals. If they can't be eaten before their expiration date, freeze them immediately. Move things closest to their expiration date to the front of your refrigerator, and keep the newer products to the back.

Think up uses for small portions, or stick leftover food into bags and freeze for later meals. Odd bits of cheese can be grated with dried breadcrumbs or crusts to use as toppings on casseroles or potatoes. Yogurt can be blended into smoothies or spooned on top of breakfast cereal for a treat.

Does your bread box contain bits of bread crusts? Try freezing them. Keep adding to your freezer stack of bread crusts until you have enough to make into bread stuffing. Or you can cube them, mix them with oil and seasonings, and toast them in the oven for salad croutons. Why buy expensive croutons or stuffing mix when you can make them at home and cut the cost? You'll find homemade to be far tastier anyway.

Internet bloggers report that they have successfully frozen eggs. A blogger from Boise, Idaho, reports that she recently bought ten dozen eggs on sale. She cracked them, placed them into ice cube trays, froze them, and then transferred them to freezer bags. Now she takes her cubed eggs out of the freezer as she needs them.

Cakes and cookies can be crumbled and sprinkled atop deserts or used as pudding toppings. Stale bread was often used by our grandmothers to make delicious bread pudding.

Even the smallest portion of leftovers can be used. Young mothers can puree small portions of meals and turn them into baby food. Small pureed portions can even be frozen in ice cube trays and placed in freezer bags as were the eggs discussed above. Homemade baby food is far less costly and far more nutritious and tasty than commercial brands.

*Take care of produce.* Citrus fruit can be squeezed and frozen before it goes bad. Green peppers can be chopped and frozen. The same goes for spinach, asparagus, and broccoli. If you see that your produce is past its prime, freeze it rather than wait for it to spoil.

For better storage, keep artichokes, asparagus (with ends cut and placed in water), beets, broccoli, cabbage, carrots, cauliflower, celery, chilies, cucumbers, eggplant, lettuce, green beans, mushrooms, and zucchini in your fridge's humidified crisper.

Store berries, citrus, corn on the cob, melons, and peas near the front of your shelves, where the temperature is warmer. Apples, cherries, and grapes can be placed anywhere in the fridge provided they don't freeze, though apples should be placed by themselves in a crisper so they won't pick up flavors from other foods.

Leave apricots, avocados, bananas, kiwis, mangos, nectarines, papayas, peaches, pears, plums, and tomatoes on the counter, where they are less likely to become subject to chill injury. Use your fresh produce first. Don't use canned or frozen vegetables until you no longer have anything fresh. Store garlic, onions, potatoes, and winter squash in a cool room.[5]

Salads and stews can be made from odds and ends of leftover vegetables. Vegetables and fruits can even be mixed together and topped with dressing.

Mash overripe bananas and use them for banana bread or banana cake. Before they get too ripe, slice them up and freeze them. Perhaps even dip them in a little chocolate. If you have a food dehydrator, dry your bananas. Our grandmothers often mashed ripened bananas and poured a little cream over the top for a lovely banana pudding.

*Look through the leftovers.* Do you have enough for a second meal? Can you take what is left to make a soup, a stew, a stroganoff, or a pasta dish? Do you have enough to make into a casserole?

Only a generation ago, our mothers and grandmothers purposely cooked a large roast, ham, chicken, or turkey and planned an entire week's meals around the leftovers. Every crumb from Sunday dinner was utilized. Today, Sunday's chicken can become chicken tacos, chicken quesadillas, chicken salad, or chicken and noodle casserole. By the end of the week, the chicken carcass can be turned into chicken stock.

It is easy to make chicken stock. Take the remaining bones, skin, and fat and place them in a large pot. Add a few carrots, a couple sticks of celery, and an onion. Add salt and pepper and a few spices—oregano and thyme work well—bring to a boil, and simmer four to six hours (all day in a slow cooker). Strain the stock when you are finished, use it right away, or freeze it for later.

One family we know made a habit of cooking a turkey every month or two. Turkey is inexpensive when purchased on sale. They ate their turkey for a meal or two and then carefully sliced what remained for turkey sandwiches. If there was any turkey remaining a day or so later, they froze it for turkey soup or turkey casserole.

You can use roast beef the same way. We've often enjoyed three or four meals from a single roast and made everything from stroganoff to vegetable soup with the leftovers.

*Maintain a well-stocked pantry.* Keep your pantry stocked with ingredients that are necessary for many and varied dishes. Keep a good supply of creamed soups, tomato soup, whole tomatoes, tomato sauce, spaghetti sauce, canned legumes, canned vegetables, and sacks of potatoes. Keep peanut butter, granulated sugar, powdered sugar, brown sugar, and spices in your storage. Store tuna and canned chicken. Keep oatmeal, cornmeal, flour, and wheat. Certain key ingredients can be turned into a number of dishes and will save you untold dollars.

To keep your pantry full, keep a notebook or a clipboard in your kitchen pantry or food storage area. Whenever you use a product, record it so it can be replaced. When it comes time to go to the store, this record becomes the beginning of your shopping list.

# Shop the Sales

One of the surest ways to save money is to buy a product only when it goes on sale. Everything eventually goes on sale. Peruse your weekly ads, and plan your menus based on the week's sale items. Keep in your head at least a basic knowledge of prices so you can distinguish between sales and featured grocery items.

Each food product has its own sales cycle. The cycle can be as short as three months or as long as a year. Some of these cycles are readily apparent; some are not. Nearly every homemaker knows that the best time to stock up on flour, sugar, and other baking items is during the holiday season. Because the holidays immediately follow the nation's harvest, grains, sugar, shortening, and other items are sold at their lowest price. Other products are not so predictable. Watch for case-lot sales featuring canned goods and soups. Even toilet paper, paper towels, and foil have their season for savings. Take a few minutes each week to peruse the ads. Do you see something you are about to run out of? Put it on your list.

After a while, shopping ads will become so routine that you will be able to assemble your shopping list quickly.

When a product is on sale, buy enough to last until it goes on sale again, particularly if it is something you use regularly. We have found a system that works well. Before you move your purchases from the bags to the shelf, take a moment to write the day's date on each can, box, or package with a marking pen. When you run out of a product, record that date in your notebook or on your clipboard. How long did it take you to use that product or finish that case of vegetables or soup? Now you have a rough idea of what your family is likely to consume in a year.

For example, if it takes two months to go through a can of peanut butter, you will need only six cans of peanut butter in your year's supply. If it takes three months to use a can of shortening, you'll need four cans of shortening to last a year. This process should consume only a few minutes of time and will become more of a routine and less of an annoyance over time.

The Internet is a handy tool for checking prices. Some regions have services to rate grocery sales. For example, the Salt Lake City region has a service available through the Newspaper Agency Corporation that analyzes grocery ads and rates sale items on a five-star system. You can find this Web site at www.gurusdeals.com. You can also search for grocery savings through the Internet. You might find a store or a generic Web site to assist you with grocery deals specific to your area or specific to your favorite grocery chain. Most major supermarkets maintain their own Web site, and large co-ops, such as Associated Foods, maintain a site for their affiliates. These sites are also available in international areas. We have found Web sites for grocery savings in the U.K. as well as in many other countries of the world.

# Plan Your Menus and Make a List

*Know what you spend on food.* For a week write down every penny you spend on food. Don't forget trips to the vending machine, stops at the convenience store, lunches out, and restaurant meals.

*Have a plan.* Plan a week's menus. A menu and a detailed list allow you to make fewer trips to the grocery store. If you can shop less frequently, say once a week or every ten days, you will save lots of money. The more often you walk into a store, the more often you will be tempted to buy things you don't really need.

As you build your menus, include a day or two of low-cost meals or leftovers. Pancakes, soups, stews, bread and milk, johnnycake with maple syrup, beanie-weenie casserole, and creamed tuna over toast are low-cost meals designed to stretch your food dollar. In less prosperous times, mothers just planned for several of these days each week. Before finalizing the menus, go over your shopping list, estimate the cost, and make adaptations to fit your budget.

One of our friends has written all of her family's favorite recipes on 3x5 cards with a list of the ingredients on the reverse side of each card. She has fastened them together with a large ring. Planning menus is easy for her. She simply flips through her rolled stack of cards, jots down meal plans, and checks the flip side for what she needs to buy.

Breakfasts and lunches offer great opportunities for savings. Keep your breakfasts simple: cooked cereal, yogurt, fresh fruit in season, and canned fruit in the winter. Lunches can be simple too: salads, sandwiches, and canned soup.

We can learn valuable lessons from our grandmothers, who likely cooked for large families during days of incredible hardship. Here is one of the ways our grandparents coped: Sunday became the biggest meal of the week simply because it was the day the entire family could be counted on to be home. Sunday meals were not just nourishment; they were family events. Only on Sunday did Mother prepare a dessert. On Monday, Mother warmed Sunday's leftovers. On Tuesday, she made soup or stew and used up all that remained of Sunday's leftovers. If there was no meat, Mother found a good soup bone and simmered it with vegetables. She supplemented Tuesday's supper with fresh biscuits or cornbread.

Wednesday was baking day. Mother made enough bread to last another week. That night she sliced hot bread fresh from the oven and placed jams, jelly, honey, and butter on the table beside the bread and a pitcher of milk. No one complained on bread-and-milk night. It was a family favorite.

Thursday and Friday were days for fresh, low-cost meals, and Saturday night the fare was always light. Every bit of leftovers was used so that the refrigerator or *ice box* was ready to receive Sunday's leftovers. Then the cycle started all over again. This was the way the woman of yesteryear fed her family for less.

## Know Your Grocery Store

Remember that grocery stores have to make a profit or they can't stay in business. That is just simple economics. However, much research and money have gone into retail marketing. It pays for you to understand marketing techniques.

*Loss leaders.* Retailers lure shoppers into their store every week by selling products at or below cost. Marketers call these *loss leaders.* If one item is sold at a loss, the retailer knows that the shopper will compensate for the store's loss on that item by buying other products at full price. In this way, the store is more than compensated for the loss leader. When you need to save money, buy only the loss leaders and the sale items.

*Shop more than one store.* Plan on hitting more than one store during a shopping session. This is only to your advantage if you live within a short distance of several markets. Remember to buy enough of the sale item to last until it goes on sale again.

*Shop on Wednesdays.* Researchers have found that Wednesdays are the least-busy shopping days of the week, and since the ads for the week usually begin on Wednesdays, stores are better stocked on that day.

*Be loyal only to price.* Forget the brand and forget the store. When it comes to grocery shopping, make price the king.

If you know a store that matches prices, head for that particular supermarket with your highlighted weekly ads. Buy what's on sale at all the stores, pull out your ads at checkout, and tell the clerk that you desire a price match.

*Do self-checkout.* When you want to limit your purchases, walk past the carts, grab a small shopping basket, and do your own checking and bagging. Researchers have found that shoppers will not place as many items in their basket when they have to do their own checkout.

*Go generic.* We've already discussed the benefits of house brands, or generics, and their price and quality. Nevertheless, many of us still buy name brands. Try an experiment. For one month buy only generic brands. Try a variety of items, and have your family taste them all and respond. Obviously, they will like some products better than others, but for every generic product they like, you'll be able to eliminate a name brand that costs more. You can save as much as several hundred dollars each year if you are willing to buy generic.

*Understand the store layout.* Stores are arranged to bog down shoppers at aisle ends, and displays are made attractive on these ends for a reason. As you slow down, displays entice you to buy items that probably aren't on your shopping list. Don't buy unless you need the item and know that it is on sale. If you are not sure, wait until you can go down the aisle where that item is displayed and compare its price with others of similar quality.

In addition, most stores carefully arrange for their staple items to be either at the far ends or at the back of the store. Store owners hope that as shoppers walk down the aisles toward the milk, eggs, bread, and produce, they will pick up several more items along the way.

Each bank of shelves is marketed to entice you to buy the most expensive brands. Brand names have brighter and more eye-catching labels. In addition, the most expensive brands are arranged at eye level, while the less expensive brands are placed on higher or lower shelves. Keep your eyes moving, and don't be lured by the most attractive labels.

*Look for unit pricing.* Many retailers place unit pricing next to their price on the shelf edge. The unit price allows you to compare cans and packages of different weights and sizes to find the most economical.

*Watch the register at checkout, and examine your receipt.* Scanning machines are highly accurate, but it still pays to watch the register for errors as items are scanned in. If you catch a mistake on the charge of an item, some stores will give you that item for free.

It's a good idea to look over your receipt before exiting. We have all seen mistakes on receipts—some in our favor, some not. If you are honest with your retailer, he will likely be honest with you.

*Nonfoods.* Today's supermarket carries far more than just food. One-stop shopping saves time but may not always save money. Personal items might be better purchased at pharmacies or discount stores or even warehouse clubs.

Cleaning solutions can be homemade at a fraction of their store price. Here are a few cleaning solutions you might consider making for yourself:

- *Triple-action multipurpose cleaner.* Pour ¼ cup baking soda, 1 cup ammonia, ½ cup white vinegar, and 1 gallon of water into a large bucket. Mix thoroughly. Store in clean bottles and use as needed.

- *Window cleaner.* Mix 1 cup alcohol, 1 tablespoon ammonia, 3 cups water, ½ cup liquid dish soap, and a few drops of food coloring, and pour into a spray bottle.

- *Carpet stain remover.* After vacuuming the affected area, cover the stain with a thin layer of baking soda and pour a little seltzer water over it. The mixture will fizz. Wipe carefully so as not to damage the carpet.

- *Hard-water stain remover for windows.* Rinse the window with plain water, spray with straight vinegar, and squeegee. The hard water stains will be gone.

- *Chrome polish.* To clean a water-spotted faucet or tap, try a little flour on the tap and rub with a dry rag. For stubborn spots or thick layers of water deposits, try trisodium phosphate. To polish a porcelain sink, use a pumice stone. Wet the stone thoroughly and rub until the stain disappears.

# General Tips

*Don't be distracted.* Listen to the music in the grocery store. It is generally soft, slow, and soothing and causes you to slow down and enjoy your shopping experience. Don't let the music cause you to lose focus. Stick to your list. Remember one of the governing rules of shopping: Leave the children at home if they distract you. Children can be budget busters.

*Don't shop when you are hungry.* When you're hungry, packaged meals and snacks become more tempting, and impulse buying becomes easier.

*Use coupons.* Some shoppers have become masters at coupon shopping. Keep an organized file of coupons, consider joining a coupon co-op to swap them, and share surplus coupons with friends and family.

Some stores carry coupons for generic or house brands. You'll find these coupons in their weekly ad or somewhere in the store. Coupons are available in newspapers, mailings, and online at such Web sites as www.smartsource.com, www.coupons.com, and www.couponmom.com. Use a coupon only if you intended to purchase that particular item anyway.

*Stretch your food.* You probably know most of these tricks, but we'll give them to you anyway. Frosted corn flakes can be mixed with regular corn flakes to significantly reduce the sugar content. More expensive chocolate milk can be diluted with regular milk without your children detecting much of a difference. Mix 2-percent milk with instant nonfat powdered milk to produce 1-percent milk. Ground meat can be mixed with legumes or ground turkey to make it stretch further. Spaghetti sauce can be enriched with onions, peppers, celery, zucchini, spinach, or other vegetables. Orange juice can be mixed with lemonade, which is less expensive, to make a delicious drink.

*Buy in bulk.* Here's where the unit price comes in handy. When you are considering buying in bulk, consult the unit price. Sometimes you'll find just what you'd expect—the bigger the box, the better the buy. On the other hand, we've sometimes seen that the smaller box or the medium-size box has the lowest price per unit.

Some items are best bought in bulk because you always need them: diapers, diaper wipes, toilet paper, soap and other toiletries, canned soups, and canned fruits and vegetables. You may initially spend more for large quantities, but you'll save more and go to the store less.

If you find a great deal, buy up and share with family and friends. If getting a good price on a roast means buying a larger one than you need for a meal, cut it in half. Cook half now and freeze the rest. If your hamburger is cheaper when you buy five pounds or more, repackage it into one-pound portions and freeze. When chicken goes on sale, buy large quantities and repackage it in freezer bags large enough to feed your family.

*Shop at a farmers' market.* The best quality produce is available at your local farmers' market. Some cities designate a central marketplace where many farmers can gather to sell their produce at harvest time. Other cities spread markets about in several locations. Produce at these marketplaces is often sold by the bushel or the box. This is the best place to find quantities large enough for home canning.

*Bring a calculator and pay in cash if you have trouble staying within budget.* Never use a credit card to pay for food unless you're willing to add interest to your grocery bill. If you use a debit card, be careful. Enter debit purchases in your check register, or keep track online.

Some families have found that the best way to stick to their budget is to take cash to the store. Leave the checkbook and the credit card at home. You'll stick to the budget because you'll have to.

*Cook from scratch whenever possible.* Bread, cookies, cakes, cereals, puddings, pies, and so forth are always better when cooked from scratch. To save time, we have sometimes taken a day or two, perhaps a Saturday, toward the beginning of the month to organize and prepackage meals for the month ahead. You can cut your vegetables, brown your meat, and assemble ingredients to place into a casserole or slow cooker. You might bake several loaves of bread if you have the time and inclination, and freeze them. Any preparation work you can do in advance and have available in your refrigerator or freezer will cut down your cooking time and will save you the price of expensive packaged foods or even eating out when time becomes a factor in meal planning.

*Plant a garden.* A vegetable garden saves money. During the Great Depression and the war afterward, people became experts at turning their yards into gardens. This practice saved many families from malnourishment and starvation.

# The High Cost of Eating Out

To suggest eating out less often to a frugal family would seem laughable, but for multitudes of families in a time-starved generation, it is no laughing matter. A 2006 study published by the U.S. Department of Agriculture conducted by Rutgers University found that almost three-quarters of the people surveyed ate out at least once a week, and 10 percent ate out almost every day.[6] The cost to American families is tremendous. The National Restaurant Association projected $565.9 billion in sales in 2009.[7] The U.S.

Department of Agriculture calculates that eating out accounts for half of total food expenditures, an increase of more than 16 percent since 1972—just one generation.

For far too many families, eating out has become a way of life. Their refrigerators and their pantries are nearly empty, and so are their pocketbooks. They are at a loss as to how to make ends meet. They know they have to make changes, but they feel powerless. Some can't even cook from scratch. Though it may seem overwhelming, cooking at home saves time and health as well as money. Consumers fail to take into account that driving to a fast-food restaurant and waiting in line may take just as long as preparing your own lunch or dinner. And we haven't even mentioned the high calorie content of fast food!

Let's compare just the savings of bringing a lunch from home with buying a lunch at work. Stacie is a registered dietitian in the Washington, D.C., area. She and her husband frequently disagree on lunch purchases. Though she works at a hospital and has ready access to a cafeteria, Stacie embarks on an experiment and chooses to pack her lunch every day for six months. She wants to prove a point to her husband—bringing a lunch from home is far less expensive than eating out. She begins her experiment by buying a lunch box at Wal-Mart for $10. Stacie's experiment went as follows:

Monday: Peanut butter and jelly sandwich on wheat bread, raw carrots, baked potato chips, and an apple.

> Peanut butter ($0.11)
> Jelly ($0.07)
> Wheat bread ($0.30)
> Raw carrots ($0.12)
> Bag of chips ($0.28)
> Apple ($0.50)
> Cost: $1.38

Tuesday: Turkey sandwich on wheat bread with lettuce, light mayonnaise, carrot sticks, canned pears in light syrup, and a snack pack of Oreos.

Turkey and wheat bread ($1.30)
Lettuce ($0.25)
Light mayo ($0.14)
Carrot sticks ($0.12)
Canned pears in light syrup ($0.69)
Oreos ($0.41)
Cost: $2.91

Wednesday: Tuna salad sandwich, banana, celery sticks with peanut butter, baked potato chips.

Tuna sandwich ($1.00)
Banana ($0.25)
Celery sticks with peanut butter ($0.25 + $0.11)
Bag of chips ($0.28)
Cost $1.89

Thursday lunch: repeat of Monday (cost: $1.38)
Friday lunch: repeat of Tuesday (cost: $2.91)

Then Stacie calculated the difference between what she would spend on lunch in a year and what her husband was spending:

Cost of eating out (average $6 per day) = $30.00 per week
Cost of packing a lunch for five days = $10.47
Total savings ($19.53 per week for 52 weeks) = $1,015.56![8]

The savings don't have to end there. Let's suppose that Stacie was able to persuade her husband to take his lunch from home and invest the difference. Obviously prices increase every year, but what if Stacie's husband were to invest $4 a day until he reaches age sixty-five? Investment returns vary, but let's suppose that Stacie and her husband are young and let's suppose that over the course of their lifetime, they invested that savings and earned an average of just 6 percent per year. By the time these two young people reached retirement age, they might have earned close to a million dollars from their savings. Is that high-cost lunch really worth losing such a tidy nest egg?

Brown-bag lunches need not be boring. A quick search of the Internet for lunch suggestions can yield some ingenious and delicious menus. All you need for haute cuisine from home is a great imagination. What's more, packing a lunch takes less time than you might think. We have packed children's lunches for years. One lunch takes less than five minutes a day, and several lunches can be prepared assembly-line style. Some organized brown baggers prepare their lunches a week at a time. Others say they like to prepare sandwiches or small meals on the weekends and take them out of their freezer every morning just before leaving for work.

Remember what we said about standing in line? Packing a lunch can save the average worker fifteen to twenty minutes a day. Less time spent on lunch might mean an earlier return home each evening and more time with the family.

For those rare occasions that you dine out, here are some suggestions for trimming costs at a restaurant:

- *Avoid appetizers, or make the appetizer your meal.* Appetizers only add cost and calories unless the appetizer becomes the meal—along with a salad, sandwich, or soup.

- *Eat desserts at home, or go to a lower-priced establishment for your dessert.* When ending a night out with friends, take them to your home for dessert.

- *Eat a snack before going out.* You'll buy less and save more.

- *Use restaurant coupons.* You can find coupons online, in the newspaper, and in entertainment booklets that offer two-for-one specials.

- *Try lunch instead of dinner.* Lunch at most restaurants is less expensive than dinner.

- *Look for new restaurants.* Newly opened restaurants often offer discounts for attracting new customers.

- *Avoid weekends.* Terrific specials and coupons are more likely to be offered during the week when fewer people eat out.

- *Drink water.* Sodas are costly. You can sometimes buy a two-liter bottle of soda at the store for the price of just one fountain drink at a restaurant.

- *Bring leftovers home.* Restaurant portions are generally twice the portion of a recommended serving; take advantage of that. Eat half and plan on taking the other half home to eat for another meal.

- *Have small children share a meal.* Since a restaurant is likely to give your small children more than they can eat, consider dividing a meal or two.

Travel time, fewer wholesome home-cooked meals, and less time around the dinner table with your family all constitute part of the high cost of eating out. So stay home, eat well, and save your money. Sounds delightful! *Bon appetit!*

As in our previous chapter on family fun, we share recipes for some of our favorite low-cost meals on our Web site: www. live4half.com.

# Chapter 6

# How to Own a Home without Its Owning You

No sentiment about home has been better expressed than the words written more than 150 years ago by John Howard Payne:

*'Mid pleasures and palaces though we may roam,*
*Be it ever so humble, there's no place like home.*[1]

Home is more than four walls, a roof, and a floor. Home is where people are bound together in love, yet nothing can be more jarring to that setting than squabbles over money. Such was the case with first-time home buyers Megan and Jason.[2]

Still in their twenties, this couple decided to plunge into the housing market. They thought they had done their homework. They researched and planned for months. They drove around from place to place trying to avoid a costly mistake. They found a small condo in a good location selling under cost. They jumped at it. They were both employed and making good wages. They thought they had made a sound decision, but two years later, after the addition of a baby and the housing market collapse, things went bad. They were still employed, but their bosses cut their hours—in half. Now the stacks of unpaid bills began to mount. Most difficult to meet were their mortgage payments. Megan and Jason had ugly arguments and harbored bitter feelings.

It is no longer easy to own a home without its owning you. The Federal Reserve reported that the 2008 collapse of the housing market plummeted net worth by more than 20 percent in just one year. In this chapter we will discuss three crucial topics: home management basics, strategies for buying a home and getting a mortgage, and dealing with the threat of foreclosure.

# Household Management Basics

It seems like only yesterday that friends talked openly of changing carpet, buying furniture, and decorating their home—not because they had to but because they were tired of what they owned. For the moment at least, those days are gone. People are learning that being satisfied with what they have is not that bad.

### Appliances—Repair or Replace?

When an appliance broke down, it used to be common practice to run right out and find the newest and greatest replacement. A good rule for today's consumer, however, is to try to fix the old appliance first and replace it *only* if necessary.

A friend owned an older model washing machine. When the clothes dryer that matched it wore out, her family and friends urged her to replace them both. She resisted, replacing only the dryer. When the new dryer developed a slight problem, she called a repairman. When he saw her washing machine, he beamed with satisfaction. "You just can't find a better model machine than that one," he told her. "Those machines never wear out and seldom need fixing. They don't make them like that anymore." She had made the correct decision.

*When to buy?* At some point the washing machine tank will corrode, the bearings on the garbage disposal will go out, the dishwasher will start to leak, and the rusty water heater will stop heating water. This is the right time to buy a new appliance.

*Consider the cost.* The first thing to do before you look for a new appliance is to consider the cost. How much are the new appliances? Consult your checking and your savings accounts to see how much cash you have on hand. Can you afford a new appliance?

*Buying used.* If you don't have enough money to buy new, then look for a good used appliance. We once bought a used refrigerator for $300 and used it for fifteen years before we had to replace it. We definitely got our money's worth. When we bought our refrigerator, it was only three years old, but we got it for one-third its original price.

*Check the classifieds.* You'll find used appliances in your newspaper's classified section, in the free want ads available in your local market, at garage sales, and on the Internet. Try your local TV station's Web site, eBay, Craigslist, and so forth.

*Buying new.* Let's say you are in a position to buy new. Begin by doing your homework. Go to a showroom and look at the various brands and models. You'll find everything from stripped-down versions to high-tech versions. Talk to several salesmen. Listen to what they tell you about the features of each brand and model so you can determine what specifications you desire. Look for the best price, the highest quality, and a good repair record. In comparing brands and models, write down the various brands, models, and specifications you desire. Then go home. Research and check ratings on the Internet. Talk to neighbors and friends, and read comments online from consumers who have already purchased the model and brand you prefer.

After you make your decision, you want to find the lowest price. Peruse newspaper ads, check online, and look through appliance showrooms. Remember to be loyal only to price.

*Extended warranties.* When you make your purchase, your salesman will undoubtedly ask if you would like an extended warranty. Most extended warranties are not worth their cost because they are seldom needed. On the other hand, the retailer stands to make 40–80 percent on each warranty. You would be better off investing the cost of an extended warranty in a savings account earmarked for repairs.

## Buying Furniture

The same rules employed in purchasing appliances can be applied to purchasing furniture. In addition, when buying a piece of furniture, consider its primary use before heading to the store. Is it going into the parlor, where it will seldom be used? In that case, attractiveness may be more important than comfort and durability. Or is it going into the room where your family hangs out? In that case, look for something that will wear like iron and still be comfortable. Examine the upholstery to ensure that it is tightly woven and able to withstand heavy wear. Avoid light colors. Will the frame withstand children? Will it be easy to clean? Will it likely fade if it is placed near a window? Consider every factor before you buy.

*Take your time.* Furniture is not frequently replaced, so take a few days to research your purchase. You may walk into a store and fall in love with something, but if you don't do your research and think it through, you may face buyer's regret.

*Outlet stores.* Don't be afraid to shop wholesale outlets and scratch-and-dent centers. We've picked up fabulous pieces of furniture at fractions of their original price by buying through outlets. A $1,000 dining room table that sells for $200 at a discount center can usually be matched with any number of clearance chairs. Furniture doesn't have to be bought in a matching set. You can mix and match and still achieve a pleasing ensemble. Look through decorating magazines for ideas before you head to the outlet center.

*Used furniture.* Used furniture is great when you can't afford new. You'll want to check those classified sources we mentioned earlier.

*Reupholster.* If you are good with your hands, consider learning how to reupholster or make slipcovers. Continuing-education centers often offer a reupholstery class. Fabric is less expensive than furniture, and when the frame of old furniture is still good, reupholstering makes your furniture appear to be brand new.

Change the pillows and the rugs, and voilà, you have a whole new look!

## Home Improvements

*Do it yourself.* According to U.S. census figures, the average home owner spends $1,500 or more per year on home improvements and repairs.[3] When possible, make your own home improvements. You can enhance your abilities by attending classes at the local hardware store, by picking up brochures, or by checking out how-to books at your local library. Look for demonstrations on video, DVD, or the Internet.

*Consult an expert.* Do you know a neighbor or friend who is good at the work you are about to tackle? Ask him over to give you advice or to inspect your work. Experts are also ready to assist you at your local home improvement center.

*Get more than one bid.* Consider only licensed professionals with good references, and ask each for a bid. Talk to their references, and check out the quality of their previous work. Many scam artists work in the construction business.

*Only add value.* Don't make renovations that add no particular value to your home. Some improvements actually decrease your home's value. Improvements to living space, particularly kitchens and bathrooms, are always valuable. Swimming pools, sports courts, and gazebos may make your home more enjoyable but may not add value to your property. Before you make an improvement, check with a realtor to see if the improvement adds value to the price of your home.

*Do routine checks, and keep up with maintenance.* Keep your furnace and air conditioner in top condition. Also check the condition of your roof and the stability of your concrete. If minor improvements and maintenance suffice, overhaul before replacing.

*Fix the plumbing when the problem is small.* Fix leaky faucets or pipes as soon as you notice a problem. If a toilet seems loose, reseal it at once before it leaks into your flooring and causes a major problem. If you notice a washing machine or a dishwasher leaking, check the pipes and stop the leak.

*Clean and maintain.* Protect your roof and landscaping from spring runoff by cleaning your rain gutters of leaves and debris. In addition, periodically have your sewer pipes cleaned. Consider having your heating ducts cleaned as well. Keep the caulking in your home in good condition. Repaint exterior surfaces before they wear, but don't repaint if a touch-up will do. Keep everything clean, attractive, and maintained. Good maintenance saves on costly repairs.

*Keep good records.* If you keep receipts for home improvements, they might just save you money on your taxes. For example, you can deduct improvements that are made to accommodate an injury, physical problem, or business need. Be sure to consult a licensed tax preparation specialist, or call the IRS before claiming home improvements as deductions.

*Take advantage of special offers.* Occasionally your local power or natural gas company will offer incentives to replace your windows or update your insulation. Visit their Web sites from time to time and check your power bills for these offers.

# Buying a Home and Getting a Mortgage

Occasionally the time arrives when we need to buy a new home. Perhaps you need additional space, perhaps you need to downsize because your children have grown and gone, or perhaps your present home has become too expensive for you to maintain. Whatever the reason, you will need a sound understanding of home-buying basics to avoid losing money.

*Rent or own?* Unless you live in a locality where renting is the norm, it is always better to own than to rent—if you can afford it. Homes are investments. They generally appreciate in value. Money expended on mortgage payments and improvements add value and are recouped at the time of sale. Most of the time, home ownership reaps more profit than loss.

*How big a home should you buy?* Determining how much home you can afford is a detailed process. Lenders can prequalify you and help you determine how much you can borrow. Before determining the highest amount a lender will allow you to borrow, he must consider the amount of your current debts. The monthly total of debt payments combined with your mortgage payment should never exceed 38 percent of your monthly gross income. Nevertheless, remember that just because a mortgage company is willing to qualify you for X dollars does not mean that X dollars is a sum you can afford. You should take into account many other factors regarding your financial situation before determining your housing budget.

Lenders will not consider the size of your family, the educational and vocational needs of your children, your charitable or missionary contributions, or other financial obligations. Nor will they consider your age or retirement needs. They do not know how secure your job is. They care nothing about family crises or other unexpected expenses. For these reasons, lower considerably any ceiling offered by a mortgage lender if you want a home you can reasonably afford.

*How to determine a monthly mortgage payment.* You might do well to play with scenarios on a mortgage calculator before you head out to prequalify. You can find such a calculator on the Web site of any lending institution. The calculator determines monthly payment information based on different types of mortgage options. We'll explain more about that later. For now, just play with figures: size of mortgage, length of mortgage, and interest rate. You'll gain at least a basic understanding by performing this exercise.

In addition to making monthly mortgage payments, a home owner will have to make prorated payments that are attached to his monthly payment. These payments cover *property taxes, homeowner's insurance, mortgage insurance,* and, sometimes, a *homeowner's association fee.* These payments collected by the mortgage company with the monthly mortgage payment are deposited into an *escrow* (noninterest-bearing) account. Your mortgage company holds these additional funds in escrow until tax and insurance payments come due, generally annually.

Property tax is assessed by the county. Homeowner's insurance, which we'll discuss in a later chapter, protects the home and valuables. Mortgage insurance is required for anyone who borrows more than 80 percent of the total value of a home. It is a protection to the mortgage company, ensuring payment in the event of the death or disability of the home owner.

Some neighborhoods or communities also assess another fee called the homeowner's association fee. This fee is generally confined to exclusive neighborhoods or communities of condos, apartments, town homes, or any other neighborhood with communal yards, gardens, recreation centers, swimming pools, golf courses, and so forth. If you are considering moving into such an area, ask about the cost of the homeowner's fees. Never allow yourself to be blindsided by fees you did not expect.

If you have a good credit rating and make a substantive down payment, and you are not a first-time home buyer, you do *not* need to have funds held in escrow. You can place them into your own interest-earning account and pay them yourself when they come due. This becomes your option when your *equity* becomes greater than 22 percent of your home's market value. Equity is the residual balance of your home's market value minus the principal portion of your mortgage. You may need to prove to your lender that you will actually pay your taxes and insurance. This is easily done. You can have your bank arrange an automatic monthly transfer of funds into a designated savings account, or you can do so yourself when you deposit your paycheck. In addition, once you meet this same qualification you can cancel your mortgage insurance policy.

## Types of Mortgages

The type of mortgage you decide upon will also influence the size of your monthly payment. Decades ago there was only one kind of mortgage—the fixed mortgage. Today there are many choices, most of which involve risk. For this reason, we want you to know mortgage basics before someone tries to talk you into something you had not bargained for.

*Fixed-rate mortgages* have been the industry standard and are the least-risky mortgage alternative. The monthly payment is fixed during the term of the loan. The house payment is stable and locked in. The only risk to a fixed-rate mortgage is that the payment stays the same even if interest rates fall. During these periods, the home owner has the option to refinance for a lower payment. Over the long haul, the fixed-rate mortgage outperforms all other types of mortgages.

Fixed-rate mortgages are available in fifteen-year, twenty-year, thirty-year, and forty-year terms. A thirty-year fixed rate is the industry standard; the other terms are just variations. The payments on the thirty-year fixed are stable, or fixed, for the entire thirty years.

You will be given an *amortization table* with your mortgage that will show you how much of each payment goes to interest and how much goes to principal. In the initial years of your loan, you will pay mostly interest and little principal. As the years go by the amount you pay in interest will decrease while the amount you pay in principal will increase. As you near the end of the term of your loan, you will pay little interest and mostly principal.

A fifteen-year fixed-rate mortgage and a twenty-year fixed rate mortgage allow you to pay off your loan in less time than a thirty-year mortgage, meaning you pay less interest over the life of the loan. However, payments on fifteen-year and twenty-year fixed-rate mortgages are higher than those for a traditional thirty-year fixed-rate mortgage.

A forty-year fixed-rate mortgage is a relatively new option. It offers even lower monthly payments, but increasing the length of your loan to forty years means increasing how much interest you pay. Ultimately, you'll add to the size of your debt. For this reason, a forty-year fixed-rate loan benefits the lender more than the borrower.

*Semiweekly fixed-rate mortgages* have the advantage of a fixed-rate mortgage, but because a home owner makes two additional house payments each year by paying semiweekly, he shortens the term of the loan and, generally, the amount of interest he pays. You can enjoy the advantages of a semiweekly fixed-rate mortgage by opting for a fixed mortgage and making two extra payments a year on a volunteer basis.

*Adjustable-rate mortgages (ARMs).* This mortgage has been around for several decades and until recently was popular. Potential home owners were encouraged and excited by the prospect of being able to buy an expensive home with lower payments. While some adjustable-rate mortgages are pegged to prime and adjust in your favor as interest rates decrease, others are not so advantageous for the consumer. It pays to read the fine print. Many adjustable-rate mortgages begin with an initial three-to-five-year lower-than-market interest rate. After that initial period, the loan's interest rate is allowed to rise to the current market rate. Despite the fact that there are legal limits to how much the rate can rise during a given year, for many novice home buyers the adjusted rate becomes far higher than expected and far more than their household can afford.

Adjustable-rate mortgages have seemed to be a good investment based on the assumption that since housing prices had not gone down a single year since the Great Depression, the value of homes would increase every year over the course of the mortgage. Therefore, if a few years later, the home owner could not meet an increased, adjusted rate, he could simply refinance. However, some uncontrolled and speculative mortgage brokers over the last decade or two lured potential home buyers into larger and larger mortgages to purchase homes they knew they could not afford. In turn, these mortgages were cut up and sold to investors and pension-fund managers, causing a wild rise in global stock markets. The inevitable happened. The housing market crashed, the price of homes plummeted, and home owners ultimately slipped into default. There was no longer an option to refinance. Foreclosures followed. The ARM, once the darling of the industry, became a dirty word to those who were adversely affected by the plummeting housing market.

Another creative financing option offered during this speculative age was the *pay-option negative-amortization ARM.* This ARM was designed to allow a home buyer to pay less than interest each month, with the unpaid interest being tacked onto the principal of his loan. The monthly payment was reduced, but the difference between what was paid and what should have been paid was added on to the loan's balance, which increased each month. This is why it is called *negative amortization.*

Also introduced during this period was the *interest-only* mortgage. An interest-only mortgage begins with a lower monthly payment, this time because the home buyer pays interest but no principal. Like the ARM, this becomes a high-risk loan. Either the terms are fixed for the holder to pay all the interest at the front of the loan, giving them little equity, or for some the interest-only loan could never be paid off during the course of their lifetime unless the principal owed increases beyond a certain percentage of the original amount of the mortgage. The interest-only loan is advantageous or disadvantageous to the consumer based upon how it is structured. Fine print is essential reading to the savvy consumer. For many, such a loan only made the lender money. Real debt became two to three times the original loan amount. By opting for a mortgage which could be paid off early, the consumer would pay far less in interest and save money. For this reason, it became a trap for the home buyer—a trap which only worsened during the current economic downturn.

In addition, there is a cross between fixed-rate mortgages and ARMs called a *hybrid mortgage.* The hybrid, in theory, should allow more stability than a traditional ARM because the house payment is not allowed to rise too steeply, but you must remain in your home at least five to seven years for this option to be advantageous.

Last of all there is something called a *balloon mortgage.* A balloon loan may look at first blush like a standard fixed-rate loan, but at some predetermined time, generally three to ten years, the unpaid loan balance has the potential of becoming due and payable. This puts the borrower in a precarious situation if there is no likelihood he can refinance.

There is another term associated with creatively financed mortgages. This is the *jumbo loan.* If a home buyer needs to borrow more than $417,000 (or as much as $729,000 in high-priced housing states such as California), the mortgage lender may consider the mortgage to be high-risk. Because of the housing market collapse, few lending institutions are willing anymore to make jumbo loans.

You may also encounter what is called a *conforming loan.* A conforming loan is a loan of less than $417,000 that is made to borrowers who have good credit and money in the bank for collateral. A conforming loan has a lower interest rate.

Primary mortgage interest can be deducted from your income taxes, but the actual tax benefit depends upon your tax bracket. In other words, you may declare all of your mortgage interest as a deduction but you will only be benefited a percentage of that amount off your tax total. Mortgage deduction is claimed on your Schedule A as part of your itemized deductions and is only a benefit *if* your total itemized deductions exceeds the current standard deduction which the IRS adjusts annually. So in reality, you may be spending a dollar to save fifteen cents if you are in the 15 percent tax bracket. In short, pay off your mortgage early and invest the savings. You can pay interest or you can collect interest, you decide.

Fixed-rate loans are the best for paying off your mortgage early, but each variation of that fixed-rate loan has its advantages and disadvantages when it comes to early payoff. If you feel you need the discipline of a higher payment to force you to pay off your loan early, then opt for the fifteen-year or twenty-year fixed. The disadvantage is that you need either a lower-priced home or a good job to afford the higher payments. Semiweekly mortgages also fall into this category, although the payments are generally not quite as high. Another potential disadvantage to the semi-weekly option is that some lenders assess the full interest price in the form of fees. If such terms are written into your mortgage agreement, there is *no* advantage to paying semiweekly.

For early payoffs, we prefer the thirty-year fixed loan for its lower payments and greater flexibility. With a thirty-year fixed, you can have all the advantages of a fifteen-year fixed simply by paying the amount you would be assessed for a fifteen-year fixed, but you do so on your terms. If you need to return to paying what you would for a thirty-year fixed, you can do so without any worry. The same is true for the semiweekly option because you can voluntarily make two extra payments a year.

Be aware of *prepayment penalties.* These are fees that are assessed if you pay off your loan too quickly and deny the lender full interest. Since prepayment penalties are not always obvious, and since most mortgage companies won't automatically tell you about them, always ask before you finalize your mortgage. Inform your lender that you intend to pay off your loan early, and ask about prepayment penalties. If you face penalties, walk away and look for a new lender.

# Prequalifying and Points

Let's talk a bit about prequalifying. Before you go out with your agent to actually look at property, it is best that you prequalify. Prequalifying means that you have given a particular mortgage institution your personal information, and the institution has let you know how much you can borrow. The institution has also given you in writing a good-faith estimate of your monthly payments. You should always prequalify before you go looking so that you can stay within your price range.

*Shop for your mortgage as carefully as you shop for your home.* You will be living with your mortgage company for a long time. You need to know if the company is reputable, if your interest rate is fair, and if the closing costs are at or below the market standard. To avoid comparing apples and oranges, ask each lender for a quote for both interest and closing costs.

Only borrow from institutions with a proven track record. If the company is new, ask for the experience of their owners and management, and ask for references. News stories abound of unscrupulous and fraudulent lenders. If you feel at all uneasy about a lender, if you feel pressure, or if you feel uncomfortable, find someone else. Ask for a list of clients, and call them. Ask if they feel that the mortgage lender has been fair and reliable. Check with the Better Business Bureau for complaints. Never feel obligated to go with the first lender you talk to.

When it comes to finalizing your loan, you may be asked about something called *points.* Points are up-front fees assessed on your loan at closing. They generally pay down the interest rate of your loan. A single point is equivalent to 1 percent of the principal of your loan. If you borrow $100,000 and you are asked to pay two points to buy down the interest rate, you will be assessed an additional $2,000 at closing. Paying points can save you money over the term of the loan. If you can't afford to pay points, you will pay a higher interest rate.

Beware of any lender who tells you he can lower your interest rate without charging points. If a loan has no points under these circumstances, then it is certain to have a higher interest rate. Most lenders who advertise no-points loans are not in a position to offer you an attractive loan.

When buying or selling, points are great negotiating tools. You can offer your buyer points to lower his interest rate, or he can ask you if you would consider paying points so that he can afford to make you a more attractive offer.

In addition to points, mortgage lenders may also charge an *application fee.* In a turbulent market where home mortgage loans are competitive, you should not have to pay either points or application fees.

*Down payments.* Most lenders require 20 percent of the price of your property as a down payment. There are, however, ways around such a large down payment, and there are special programs available through the government for first-time home buyers. You might also meet the qualifications of a Federal Housing Administration loan or of a Veterans Association loan, which provide better terms and lower down payments.

Other solutions for down payments might be to secure a down payment loan from a private party, such as a parent or other family member. If you need to get a loan for your down payment and if your private party agrees, offer to pay back the loan with higher interest than the lender is earning on savings.

You might also find a seller or a developer who advertises that he is willing to sell for as little as 5–10 percent down, or you might find a developer or a seller who is open to *sweat equity*. Some mortgage lenders get around the down payment by arranging two loans for you—one for the down payment and the other for the remainder of the mortgage. Just be sure one of those loans is not an ARM, which you may not be able to pay in a few years.

# Finding a Suitable Residence

Here are a few other things you can do before you buy a home that will probably save you money in the long run:

- Clean up your credit, and pay off as many debts as you can.

- Don't limit the area of your search. Be willing to live in a lower-priced neighborhood where equivalent homes are being sold for lower prices than in trendy neighborhoods.

- Inquire about the sale prices of other homes in your vicinity.

- Secure a trustworthy agent, and work with and listen to your agent.

- Bargain hard. Don't let emotions take over your negotiations. Keep a cool head.

- Research the neighborhood. Once you have decided upon a home, call on a few neighbors and get a feel for the community you are moving into. Ask about schools, property taxes, and utilities.

- Get an inspection. Have an expert or series of experts check on the condition of the roof, foundation, heating and cooling system, wiring, and plumbing. Also check for dry rot and pest problems. Request a one-year warranty to secure your investment.

- Consider negotiating closing costs. Although tradition dictates what the buyer and seller generally pay, all things are open to negotiation.

- Consider charging interest to the seller on your deposit. If the seller knows he has to pay interest on your deposit, he may speed up the sale of his property. If you can help it, don't buy during a seller's market. If you do, you will pay more than you need to. If interest rates are high or if inflation is running in double digits, sit out the market until they return to reasonable levels.

- Most important, *buy only what you can afford.*

If you are the seller, here are some additional tips:

- Don't let an agent charge you more than the current standard commission. Shop around for the best terms from a variety of agents. In addition, don't allow any one agent too long a listing time. Offer a three-month listing and offer to renew it if you like the job the agent is doing.

- Fix up your home to make it more attractive. Repaint, recarpet with neutral colors, and fix anything that is broken. Remove hard-water stains. Make improvements that are cost-effective—those things that increase the price someone might pay for your house.

- Be willing to drop the price. If you are serious about selling, make the price of your home attractive. Sometimes we are not the best judge of our property because of our emotional attachment. Ask for and take the advice of your agent.

*Look at a variety of neighborhoods and compare.* You need to look at values on properties in a variety of neighborhoods as you start your search. Are the values of properties in these areas stable? Are there a lot of foreclosures? Will you get a good return on your investment if you have to sell in a few years? These are some of the questions you must ask. In addition, investigate the schools, the proximity of shopping, the cost of utilities, and the price of insurance because even insurance rates can vary from neighborhood to neighborhood.

*Use a real estate agent.* Unless you are knowledgeable about home prices, values, mortgage lenders, housing laws, negotiations, and a variety of other housing-related factors, a real estate agent is the only way to go. You could do it yourself, but it may end up costing, not saving, you money.

# Closing Costs

To complete your mortgage transaction, you will have to pay closing costs. (There are closing costs even in a refinance.) These costs are either added to the principal of your loan or are paid at the time of closing. We have already mentioned some of these costs, but for your review, here they are again:

- *Application and processing fees.* These are the costs of your paper work. They are charged either at the initiation of the loan or at closing.

- *Credit report.* You are required to pay your mortgage lender the cost of obtaining your credit report. The lender must assess whether you will be a good risk. This is not his fee to pay; it is yours. To make your credit report as clean as possible, take care of any late fees or nonpayment reports that could show up on your credit report before you apply for a loan.

- *Appraisal.* This fee is generally paid by the seller, who is charged for an appraiser to evaluate the value of the property. An appraisal can cost as much as several hundred dollars.

- *Title and escrow charges.* You will be charged for title insurance, which is required by law. The state needs to assess whether your property is free from liens or other charges against it. In addition, if escrow accounts must be set up for deposits, insurance, property taxes, or your payment to the seller, such fees become part of the closing costs.

To get a clearer picture of the total of your closing costs, ask your lender to provide you with an itemized statement before your appearance at closing.

# Refinancing

If you are thinking of selling your home to reduce your expenses, first look into refinancing as an option. If the current interest rate has dropped low enough below the interest rate you are paying to make a difference in your budget, refinancing may be a good option to lower costs.

Here's a good rule of thumb to decide if refinancing is the option for you. For every $10,000 of principal, a 0.5 percent reduction in the interest rate saves $41 a year, or $3.40 a month in interest. If you have a $100,000 mortgage, the savings is $408 a year, or $34 a month in interest. Use this base to calculate your savings. In addition, if you could be moving within the next few years, add the cost of the closing fees in your calculations. If the money you will expend in closing fees exceeds your savings should you have to sell in a few years, it is not worth refinancing.

Before leaving the subject of refinance, we warn against a common practice—refinancing as a way to eliminate debts. For years many home owners have been able to refinance their mortgage and increase its size by borrowing against the equity, or the rise in their home's value. Some have refinanced multiple times, always adding to the principal of their loan. The reality is that they are now paying for the lunch they put on their credit card over a thirty-year term, and they are risking the security of their home as a result. We are not saying you should never refinance to consolidate debts, but don't use refinance as a way to consolidate debt if you can avoid it.

# Foreclosure

In turbulent times, this matter must be addressed. Preventing foreclosure is a must. If you are in too deep, you need to read our chapters devoted to that subject. You may also need the advice of an accredited debt-counseling service.

At the first sign of trouble, here are your options:

- *Protect your credit score.* Try hard not to skip payments or pay late.

- *Prioritize your bills.* When money is not sufficient to cover your costs, pay first those bills that are most necessary for your family such as food, shelter, utilities, and taxes.

- *Don't be scammed.* People in desperate circumstances are fodder for predatory lenders or phony counselors. Do your homework by checking with the Better Business Bureau and following the tips in chapter 15 for finding a good debt counselor.

- *Call for help.* If you can't make a payment, call for help immediately. Don't make the situation worse by trying to deny it. Tell the bank as soon as you are thirty to sixty days late—while you still have options. The lender should work with you or with a certified counselor to resolve your problems. Banks do not like foreclosure any more than you do.

- *Work with your lender.* Many lenders will work with you if you submit to them a letter of hardship. They can offer you a lower-interest loan to lower your monthly payments, they might just offer lower payments on a temporary basis while your hardship exists, or they can offer a repayment agreement for the payment of delinquencies. Always accept the terms offered by your lender if you can, and then meet the terms of your agreement.

If the situation should become more serious, here are additional options:

- *Short sales.* If you have some equity but not enough to pay all the costs of selling your home, your lender may agree to delay foreclosure to give you time to sell your home. If you receive less from the sale than what you owe on your loan, this is a short sale and is subject to the lender's approval. Work out a preforeclosure sale with your lender. A short sale is better than a foreclosure, but it will still damage your credit. If the lender forgives the money you owe him following a short sale, he must report the difference to the IRS. It is considered a gift, and you will be subject to taxes as if you had earned it unless the government passes legislation for foreclosure relief. Before taking this option, also consult a tax adviser.

- *Deed-in-lieu of foreclosure.* If you have exhausted all your resources and there is no other alternative, you have the option of offering the lender a deed-in-lieu of foreclosure. This method allows you to give the lender the deed and the keys to your home. You move out, and the lender forgives the debt. Such an arrangement will, of course, hurt your credit rating, but it is not as bad as foreclosure. You should realize that mortgage lenders do not have to agree to a deed-in-lieu of foreclosure, and for legal reasons it may not be an advantage to them. They may turn you down; however, if they agree, the process will save them money in legal fees. Just as with a short sale, the lender must report the amount of money left on your loan to the IRS, and the IRS will consider it income. You may be expected to pay taxes, depending upon current legislation that relates to foreclosure relief. Again, first be sure to talk to a tax adviser, who would be aware and up to date on current tax laws.

Sometimes there are simply no options that can relieve your trial. Despite a short sale or the surrendering of your home through a deed-in-lieu of foreclosure, your lender might not even mention during negotiations that he still might sue you. He is legally entitled to what is called a *deficiency judgment* against you for any money his institution loses in the sale or surrender of your home. Generally, lenders are not so callous as to seek such legal judgments under trying circumstances from people who have tried to be honest and ethical. They also do not seek them if they know you probably don't have any money, but this remains their legal option. Do your homework. Check with the Better Business Bureau, the Department of Commerce, the Division of Real Estate, and the Bureau of Consumer Protection to learn all you can about the people or businesses you are or potentially will be working with when you face foreclosure.[4]

In conclusion, it is a trying and heart-wrenching thing to go through financial peril. Seek the help of professionals and consider every available option. Remember always to remain honest and up-front. Above all, counsel with your ecclesiastical leaders and with the Lord, and follow their advice before you make any firm decisions.

# Chapter 7

# How to Keep the Lights On

When energy supplies dwindle and costs rise, the frugal family knows that it pays to be energy conscious. Utility bills *can be* lowered, and your family *can save* hundreds of dollars as a result.

## Electricity and Natural Gas

*Cut back on big energy guzzlers.* The first step in energy conservation is to cut back on the biggest energy users first and then work down to the smaller ones. Which appliances have the biggest impact on your electric bill?

Air conditioning and heating: 29.6 percent
Refrigerator/freezer: 21.8 percent
Lights: 14.3 percent
Range/oven: 11.5 percent
Dryer: 10.3 percent
TV: 5.1 percent
Dishwasher: 3.4 percent
Computer: 2.9 percent
Washer: 1.1 percent.[1]

Therefore, by turning up your thermostat in the summer and

lowering it a few degrees in the winter, you will save on your power bill.

*Plug appliances into a power strip.* You may not realize it, but some electronics, like TVs, DVD players, and CD players continue to use small amounts of electricity even when they are not in use. You might consider plugging these appliances into a power strip that can easily be turned off when not in use. Small amounts of wasted electricity cost consumers about $3 billion annually.

*Keep the laundry room door shut.* Keep your laundry room door shut while the dryer is in use. A dryer uses air to dry the clothes. By keeping the door open you force your dryer to work harder— not to mention your air conditioner.

*Replace your dryer hose.* Replace your dryer's flexible plastic hose with a rigid but not corrugated four-inch metal duct. The rigid duct creates less airflow resistance and will allow your dryer to dry more efficiently. This simple step will save you $10 to $14 a year.

*Clean your lint trap.* Clean the lint from your dryer's lint trap every load. You'll use 50 percent less energy.

*Don't overload.* An overloaded dryer cannot work efficiently. Limit the size of your dryer's load. Not only will it take less time to dry, but also your clothes will come out less wrinkled.

*Compare costs.* Compare the cost of gas appliances with electric. Use the energy sources that are most cost-effective for your community.

*Use cold water.* Eighty-five percent of the electricity we use to wash clothes goes to heating the water. To save electricity, use cold water. Today's washing machines and their detergents are designed to perform in cold water as well as they do in hot. Switching from hot water to cold water will cut your energy consumption in half, leading to significant savings.

*Switch to compact fluorescent lighting.* Change all of your incandescent light bulbs to compact fluorescent lighting. The bulbs cost more but pay for themselves within a year because they use fewer amps and last ten times longer. In addition, according to *Kiplinger's,* "if every U.S. household replaced just one incandescent bulb with a CFL, the emissions savings would be comparable to taking three million cars off the road for a year."[2]

*Keep refrigerators and freezers clean.* Clean the coils behind or underneath your refrigerator and freezer with a tapered appliance brush to keep it running efficiently. Occasionally, pull your appliance out and vacuum the coils.

*Replace energy-guzzling appliances.* If your utility company offers rebates to customers who replace old appliances with energy-efficient models, take advantage of the offer. Some states even offer periodic "tax holidays" to purchase energy-efficient appliances.

*Turn down your water heater.* Lower your water heater temperature from 140 degrees to 120 degrees, and insulate hot-water pipes. This can save up to 5 percent of your energy bill.

*Keep your water heater free of sediment.* Drain a bucket's worth of water from your water heater a few times a year to remove sediment and increase efficiency.

*Celebrate the holidays with LEDs.* String LED lights during the Christmas season. They last longer and can save up to $11 a season.

*Limit the effect of power bumps.* Purchase an uninterruptible power system with a battery backup for your computer. It cuts down on power bumps. Because you pay on amps used and not on voltage, those bumps spike your electric meter and cause you to spend more than is necessary.

*Turn off the lights.* Train yourself and teach your children to turn off lights, television, curling irons, and other appliances when not in use.

*Consult your energy company.* Check with your local utility company for pamphlets on even more ways to save. Many companies include energy-saving tips with their monthly statements.

# Heating and Cooling

*Bring in a professional energy auditor.* Some utilities and community groups will perform the audits for free or at a nominal fee. Volunteer organizations also provide audits. They will test your home for areas of greatest heating and cooling loss, analyze your past utility bills, and estimate how long it might take to recoup the cost of upgrades to your systems. You can find certified professionals by checking www.resnet.us.

*Check the SEER.* Before buying an air conditioner or furnace, check the unit's seasonal energy-efficiency ratio (SEER). An increase of each rating point results in 10 percent more efficiency.

*Get the right furnace and air conditioner.* Owning a system that is too powerful for your home is as inefficient as owning one that is too weak.

*Tune up your furnace.* Tune up your furnace every two years. Tuning up your furnace cuts about 10 percent off your heating bills.

*Replace your furnace filters.* Check the filters monthly during winter. If you cannot see daylight through the filter, it is time to replace it. Using clean filters increases the life of your furnace fan and keeps your house warmer.

*Insulate.* You may think your home is already properly insulated, but blown-in ceiling insulation compacts over time. If your attic has less than six inches of insulation, it probably needs more. Some utility companies offer rebate programs to assist you in properly insulating your home. New insulation will eventually pay for itself through lower heating and cooling bills.

*Caulk.* Caulk air leaks that add to your heating and cooling costs. Caulk around windows, doors, near the attic, where wires and cables enter the house, and around electrical outlets. Sealing these leaks can save between 10 and 20 percent of your energy total.

*Weatherproof your doors.* Install door sweeps or weather stripping. It's the surest way to seal gaps between rooms and from the outside of your home.

*Clean vents.* Clean your vents, radiators, or baseboard heaters. If your heating and cooling systems are free of dust and grime, they will run more efficiently.

*Open blinds.* Approximately 10–25 percent of your home's heat loss comes from your windows. Open curtains, shades, and blinds on south-facing windows during the day to let light in to heat the house, and close them at night to keep it warm. On summer's hottest days, close the blinds to keep it cooler.

*Use a programmable thermostat.* Programmable thermostats adjust your heating and cooling temperatures automatically. Set temperatures higher or lower, depending on the season, when you are home, and when you are asleep. You will save up to 3 percent of your heating and cooling bill per degree lowered or raised, depending upon the season.

*Use humidifiers.* Humidifiers can reduce your winter heating costs. Moist air retains heat better than dry air, and moist air helps those with dry skin and breathing problems.

*Use ceiling fans.* Use ceiling fans to circulate the air. They work both in summer and winter to keep your home at a more even temperature. Adjust the fans to blow down in summer and up in winter.

*Close up rooms.* Keep doors closed, and close vents when a room is not occupied.

*Plant shade trees.* Trees add beauty and keep your home cool in the summer.

# Sewer

*Clean lines.* Keep your sewer lines free from tree roots. Be aware of any obstacles that might plug your system.

# Telephone

*Shop for the best service.* Prices of long distance and local dialing can be conveniently compared online, and many Internet phone services are becoming as reliable as your local utility. Computer phone service can be purchased by a simple flat fee. Before switching, check reliability either online, through consumer reports, or wherever customers can rate reliability and clarity.

*Eliminate the extras.* When money is tight, cut out extra services you don't really need.

*Look for bundled services.* Phone companies and cable providers both offer bundled services. Find the best available package that fits your needs.

*Mind your minutes.* On cell phones, your minutes count. Track them carefully, and adjust your plan to fit your needs. Though it costs more to purchase a greater number of minutes, overages will outpace the price of a plan with sufficient minutes.

*Try a prepaid cell phone.* If you are finding it hard to keep track of minutes, try a prepaid cell phone. When your minutes are gone, so is your service.

*Texting.* You can buy unlimited text service, but if you don't text that much, it may not be worth the price.

*Family plans.* Look for family plans if you have a big family and can utilize in-network calling.

*Employee discounts.* Take advantage of employee discounts on phone service if your company offers them.

*Check your statement.* Check your invoice. It may be confusing, but it is important to read and understand the charges so you can adjust your bill and check for errors.

# Water

*Take short showers.* Take short showers instead of baths. The average bath requires much more water than a short shower.

*Install low-flow showerheads.* Install a low-flow showerhead and save as much as $150 a year.

*Wash full loads.* Save water by washing only full loads in your dishwasher and clothes washer.

*Check for leaks.* Leaky faucets cost you a lot of money. Fix them immediately, and check for toilets that won't turn off. Running toilets can waste dozens of gallons of water a day. Identify leaks by listening or by adding food coloring to the toilet tank. If the color shows up in the bowl without the toilet being flushed, you have a leak.

*Sweep.* Sweeping or air blowing is more energy efficient than spraying with a hose.

*Keep the grass higher.* Keep your grass higher to preserve moisture during the hottest part of the summer.

*Mulch.* If you mulch planting areas, you can water less often.

*Water just enough.* If your grass turns a dull grey-green, it needs more water. If walking on it leaves footprints, it needs water. Be careful not to water too much.

*Water in the cool of the day.* Water during the evening or early morning. Water applied during the hottest part of the day evaporates.

*Use drip irrigation.* Install drip irrigation in your garden. You'll cut water usage and weed growth.

# Chapter 8

# How to Keep Your Car from Driving You to the Poorhouse

There can hardly be a person alive who has not seen the precipitous rise in gas prices. Even when a temporary downturn in the price at the pump allows us to breathe a little easier, we anticipate that prices will eventually rise again. The problem is that price hikes never end at the pump. An increase in the price of gasoline affects the price of just about everything else. What's a family to do in a world so dependent on automobiles?

*Buy a new car?* You could consider buying a new, economical car, but spending an additional $20,000 to buy that vehicle would save you only about $1,000. It would take twenty years just to break even. Thankfully, there are less radical ways to save money during a pump pinch.

*Plan your trips.* Instead of hopping in the car every time you need a loaf of bread, try planning trips and buying more. For a week, log every trip you make, and at the end of the week, evaluate. Which trips can be eliminated and which consolidated with others? Before taking off on the next trip, chart where you need to go and plan how you can drive there in the least amount of miles. There are some places you absolutely must go—to work, to school, and to the doctor. Everything else is flexible. Plan around those necessary trips, and run your errands while you are already out. Stop at the businesses and stores along your route, and plan detours that are not too far removed from your regular route. There are patterns to the places you frequent; take full advantage of them.

*Use public transportation.* If you are fortunate enough to live in a city with public transportation, use it. If you can access the system through your employer, all the better. You might be able to pay for your transportation in pretax dollars and save nearly a third of the expense. Call your benefits department to see if this is an option for you.

*Drive your most economical car.* Park your gas-guzzler and use it only on special occasions, such as when you take your family to church or on an outing.

*Buy regular gas if possible.* Today's cars are designed to run smoothly and resist engine wear on regular gasoline. The difference between regular and premium gasoline is the octane level. Regular gasoline usually has an octane rating of 87, mid-range gasoline has a rating of 89, and premium gasoline has a rating of 91 or 92. Octane has nothing to do with fuel power or cleanliness; it only increases the engine's ability to resist knocking or pinging, which happens when the fuel-air mixture ignites abnormally and creates a less-efficient explosion. Modern cars have sensors that regulate the knocks and pings. That is why today's cars do not require premium gasoline as they used to. Generally, only high-performance vehicles equipped with superchargers or turbochargers require high-octane gas.

*Seek the lowest-price stations.* When gas prices are high, radio stations and newspapers sometimes carry a feature to tell you where you can find the lowest prices of the day. Discount warehouse stores such as Costco or Sam's Club offer gasoline to their members at a discount. Current EPA regulations mandate detergent additives to keep your engine running clean. Don't buy into clever advertising.

*Consider a credit card with incentives.* Since most pumps operate today on credit or debit cards, you might consider using a card that offers incentives. Remember that this works only if you can pay the card in full before the due date. Carry-over credit charges on gasoline increase the price you are already paying at the pump.

*Check your tire pressure.* Underinflated or worn tires can add 2 percent more to your fuel costs for each pound they are under pressure.

*Don't let your gas tank dwindle to empty.* Most experts will tell you that with today's fuel-injection systems, your engine will perform at greater efficiency when it is half full.

*Don't top off the tank.* Reactivating a fuel pump in short bursts actually increases the likelihood that the pump will falsely record the amount of gas dispensed.

*Change the oil, spark plugs, and filters.* Keeping your engine in tip-top condition decreases fuel consumption.

*Examine your gas cap.* Make sure your cap fits tightly, and check for signs of wear. A faulty gas cap causes evaporation.

*Lighten your load.* For every one hundred pounds of weight, your fuel efficiency declines by as much as 2 percent. Look in your trunk. Are you carrying around things that do not need to be there?

*Slow down.* Reducing your speed from 70 mph to 65 mph saves 7 percent per gallon.[1] The faster you go, the more air your vehicle has to push.

*Don't race the engine.* When the traffic light turns green, don't take off like a hornet. Press slowly and evenly on your gas pedal, and brake gently. If you have a tachometer in your car, watch it for anything erratic and slow down. Erratic acceleration and quick stops add 35 percent to your energy costs.

*Don't tailgate.* Your mother always told you not to drive too closely to the car ahead, but did you realize that this is not only a matter of safety but of economy as well? Every time the driver ahead taps his brakes, you have to slow down faster than he did. That's because you have to allow time for yourself to react to his action. Hang back, and you'll drive more smoothly and use less fuel.

*Don't worry about turning off the engine.* You have probably heard that you waste gasoline every time you restart the engine, but that is no longer the case. Our modern, fuel-injection engines use little extra gas to restart; idling uses far more.

*Check your owner's manual.* Consult your owner's manual to maintain maximum fuel efficiency and a regular maintenance schedule. Your owner's manual is full of useful information. Read it.

*Hoof it or ride your bike.* You'll not only save dollars but also shed pounds.

## Save on Costly Car Repairs

Regular maintenance and tune-ups save money on fuel consumption and extend the life of your car. Make it routine to check the oil at regular intervals, and change the oil and oil filter on a regular basis. Take care of your tires, and have the brakes checked regularly. Examine the belts and the radiator hoses, and replace them before they break. Read your manual and check the systems of your car at the recommended intervals.

*Learn to do basic repairs.* If you are at all handy, you can learn to do simple repairs on your automobile. If you need help, go to the library and look for books that can teach you some repair basics.

When you need a mechanic, don't hesitate to shop around and ask for estimates. If you find a reliable and fair mechanic, stay on friendly terms with him. Don't let anyone begin a major repair on your car without first calling you with an estimate. And beware! Some shops will quote one price and charge a higher one. Honesty is one of the best characteristics of a good mechanic. Insist that the shop adhere to the estimated price of the repair. Question any costs that you feel are excessive.

*Buying tires.* Extend the life of your tires by having them rotated and balanced, and keep the wheels aligned. Keep the air pressure in your tires at the recommended level.

When it comes time to buy new tires, check prices and research brands. Some brands of tires wear better than others. Consult consumer guides either at the library or online to determine the best buy. Never buy a tire with a mileage warranty that exceeds the time you intend to drive your car, and watch the proration on your warranty. Too many times we have discovered that by the time we needed the warranty, it was worth only a few dollars off the purchase of new tires.

*Warranties.* Warranties are also offered for batteries, mufflers, shock absorbers, and brakes. Watch again for prorated warranties. Keep your car's warranties together in a handy place.

*Hang on to your car as long as possible.* Contrary to popular opinion, it is not necessary to own the latest model. Cars manufactured from the late 1980s to the present are, for the most part, reliable cars. The median age of a car on today's roadways is nine years. Better engineering and better construction of the car body make today's cars last longer than in the past. Some cars can be safely driven for more than 200,000 miles. In addition, with the median price of a car now exceeding $24,000, it makes sense to hang onto a car in good working order as long as possible.

# Buying a New Car

The time will come when the service and maintenance of your vehicle exceeds the monthly cost of buying another car. This is the time to purchase a new car. Few experiences can cause more stress than finding yourself in the automobile market. It doesn't have to be that way if you follow a simple step-by-step process.

*What do I need?* The first question you must ask yourself before you head for the car lot is "What do I really need?" How big do you need your car to be to safely accommodate your family? What extras are necessary, and which are frivolous? How much can you afford to spend? A lot of car shoppers buy bigger, fancier, and pricier automobiles than they really need.

*New or used?* New cars have the advantage of having only one owner—you. With a new car you don't inherit someone else's problem. However, a new car depreciates rapidly—starting the minute you drive it off the lot. The most cost-effective automobile is one that is between two and four years old. By that time the depreciation rate has leveled off, and the car has begun to hold its value.

*Consult reliability reports.* Before you head to the lot, narrow your choices to a make and model that has a safe and reliable track record.

*Check on insurance rates.* The price of the car is only part of the cost. What is the price of insurance on the make and model you are looking for? Talk to your insurance agent, and tell him which makes and models you are considering. Ask his advice. Avoid cars that are costly to insure. High insurance rates reflect the safety record of the vehicle.

*Shop a variety of dealers.* Don't buy the first car you see. Take a thorough look around. Give yourself plenty of choices before you narrow them down. See a lot of dealers and owners (if this is a private sale) to get a feeling for honesty and integrity.

*Buy only from a reputable seller or dealer.* Honesty and candidness are the best qualities in car dealers. You should feel comfortable with the dealer or seller you are working with. A bad feeling is an indication that you should walk away.

There are certain signs that show whether a seller is dishonest. If he greets your phone call with "What car are you asking about?" and then appears not to know much about the vehicle's history and performance and if he is reluctant to give you a name and does not indicate that he is a dealer, then you could be talking to a car thief. If you decide to buy a car but the title is not in the seller's name, the car might be stolen. Ask the seller how he acquired the vehicle. Test his honesty. Ask questions you know he should answer if he is the owner, and see how he responds. Never meet a seller at a strange location or if he seems reluctant to meet you at his home. Last of all, if the seller is reluctant to let you take the vehicle to a mechanic, walk away.

Let a dealer know up front that you are only shopping and that you will return once you have narrowed your search. Not appearing too eager lessens the pressure on you.

*Decide on one or two.* When you've narrowed your search to the top one or two cars, it is time to do some homework. Use this handy checklist and go to work:

1. *Check out the VIN.* Each car has a vehicle identification number. If you know your car's VIN, then a simple trip to the Internet will reveal your car's history.

2. *Examine the odometer.* Do the numbers on the odometer line up? Are they crooked or loose? If so, walk away. They may have been tampered with. Look at the door frames for oil and maintenance stickers, and check the glove compartment and under the hood for service records. If the stickers and the records do not correlate with the mileage on the odometer, the car has been tampered with.

3. *Ask for warranty records.* With a VIN you may be able to find repair records from a dealer. This is also a good way to verify mileage. What work has been done on the car and how often that work has been done are good indications of the vehicle's reliability.

4. *Do a thorough examination.* Does the pedal look worn? If so, it could have been mistreated or the car could have been driven more than the odometer indicates. Is the paint even, and do the body parts line up evenly? If not, this could be an indication that the car might have been in an accident. How does the car look under the hood? Do the doors, hood, and trunk open and close freely, and do the bumpers sit squarely on the frame? If not, the frame could be bent. Do you smell unusual odors? Is the inside musty or damp smelling? Do dash instruments show signs of moisture? Is there rust or mud? Does the carpet appear newer than the rest of the car? These are red flags. If you see these things, walk away.

5. *Take the car to a mechanic.* If everything checks out, take

the car to your favorite mechanic and have him look it over and test drive it. He works on cars every day; he can spot a lemon.

You are now ready for the next step, but don't get in too big a hurry. Ask for the blue book price or find it online. How does it compare to the asking price? Use your best negotiation skills and seek the lowest mutually agreeable price. Wait out your salesman. Don't be afraid to walk away if you don't like the terms, even if you come back later. If your salesman asks you for a deposit before telling you the lowest price, walk away.

*Frivolous options and extended warranties or service contracts.* Dealers make profit on the extras they sell you, so buy only what you can afford and what you feel has value. When it comes time for an extended warranty or service contract, ask to see the full contract and ask for time to look it over and think about it. If the dealer says he needs a decision right away, then don't buy the contract. If the dealer tells you to take your time, then as you look through the contract ask questions: What is covered? What is excluded? Some extended warranties are so pricey that an identical amount of money set aside in an interest-bearing account would cover the cost of a major repair.

*Pay cash if you can.* In our last book, *Debt-Free on Any Income,* we recommended that you only buy cars you can afford and that you pay yourself a car payment each month so that the money is there when you need to buy a new car. Cash is always preferable to a loan because you save on interest.

*If you have to get a loan, shop for it.* You might even want to shop for the financing before you shop for the car. This will help you narrow your choices. The best terms for a loan may not always be at a dealership. Suppose that a manufacturer is offering an incentive: a $500 rebate on a five-year loan at 4.9 percent or a $750 rebate with no financing. You want the best deal, so you speak with several lenders. The best terms you can arrange are 5.5 percent on a three-year loan. That doesn't sound as good as the dealer's offer, but which would actually be your best option? Believe it or not, your best deal would be the $750 rebate with your own financing. In other words, opt for the 5.5 percent interest rate. Many auto manufacturers have been offering a 0 percent APR to entice new buyers. What this means is that they are offering an interest-free loan in lieu of the rebate. In reality, the rebate that manufacturers extend is precisely equivalent to the interest they might have received on the loan had you obtained your financing through them and paid your car off over five years. But the manufacturer is actually gambling. Since the average owner keeps his car only two to three years (not five), the manufacturer makes more profit if he offers financing rather than extending a rebate. If the car buyer keeps the car more than five years, however, then he comes out ahead with financing from the manufacturer. The bottom line is this: The 0 percent financing makes sense if you intend to keep the car for five years, but you are also taking a gamble.

To obtain the absolute best loan possible, you should look not only for the best interest rate but also for the fewest number of years possible on your loan. Some shoppers finance their cars over more years so they can afford a higher-priced vehicle with lower monthly payments. Is this wise? No. You will spend far more money over the term of the loan than you should. It is better to buy a lower-priced vehicle and pay it off in three years than a higher-priced one spread over a five-year payment cycle. By the time you get to the end of the five years, 90 percent of the time you will owe more money on the vehicle than it is worth. Most important, never succumb to pressure from any person along the buying chain. Go slow and be sure. You can buy a good, dependable vehicle and find great satisfaction if you spend sensibly.

# Chapter 9

# How to Have a Smashing Wardrobe without Smashing Your Wallet

Clothing for your family is one of those necessary expenses, but we generally purchase clothing for more money than is necessary. The price of clothing doesn't have to overwhelm your budget.

*Buy simple, classic designs.* Trendy clothes go in and out of fashion almost seasonally, but classic clothing lasts for years. To save money, remember to buy without logos or obvious brand names. Stay away from designs and textures. Buy solid colors, particularly neutral colors like navy, black, or grey. Collars should be a medium size because big collars and narrow collars go out of style quickly.

*Mix and match.* Buy several tops or shirts and several skirts or pants in colors that complement one another and will not go out of style. In pants avoid large cuffs or flared legs; in skirts avoid fringe, large designs, and bright colors that are hard to match. Buy ties, belts, shoes, sport coats, scarves, and jewelry to change your look. Clothing that is interchangeable is as serviceable on dress-up days as it is on casual days by the change of a skirt, top, shirt, or pants.

*Stick to quality shoes.* Quality shoes are not necessarily expensive shoes. Reasonably priced shoes of superior quality can be worn several times a week for five years or more without wearing out. Buy neutral colors that are complementary, and avoid extremes such as long, tapered toes or clunky, square ones. Polish your shoes regularly to keep them looking better and lasting longer.

*Buy good quality items.* Sometimes quality *is* a bit more money, but cheap needs to be replaced too quickly. For example, a wrinkle-free, wash-and-wear, button-down shirt will last several years while a poorly made shirt will yellow and wear out quickly. In addition, wrinkle-free is more convenient and does not require special washing or ironing.

*Build classic wardrobes over time.* Quality, timeless clothing lasts so long and is so versatile that you can continue to expand your wardrobe with interchangeable pieces for many years. Eliminate things only when they become too worn to wear.

*Shop consignment stores and thrift stores.* A television news anchor once let us in on the secret of a smashing wardrobe: "I only buy from consignment stores, Deseret Industries, and Goodwill. In fact, I am not alone. Everyone in television does the same." There are great deals on gently used and even new clothing at used clothing outlets. Sometimes the original owner bought the outfit and never wore it. It may still even have the original price tag attached. Sometimes the owner grew out of it or maybe just got tired of it after wearing it once or twice. Whatever the reason, there are tremendous bargains at consignments and other used clothing outlets if you are patient. No one knows or cares where you bought your clothing.

*Look for outlet stores.* Some shopping centers specialize in the outlet stores of big chain retailers. These stores specialize in overstocks and clearances. Here you can buy at a fraction of the retail price.

*Buy out of season.* Expert shoppers tell us that they shop only at end-of-season sales. They walk into exclusive stores, walk right past the newest merchandise, and head straight for the clearance rack. To make the purchase even better, they go into the store only on special sales days when an additional 25 to 50 percent is taken off an already discounted price. Some of these same people have discovered a way to know when the price of a clearance item is at its lowest. They look for a variance in the typical marking system. Most stores price their clothing just under the whole dollar—$4.99 rather than $5. When the price is lowest, however, they mark items with an *out-of-the-ordinary number*—say, $4.97. In addition, bargain shoppers make friends with the clerks, as we advised in chapter 1. Friendly clerks will tell you when the store will be doing their markdowns. If you need new clothing, that will be the day for the best prices.

Let's give you an example of how well this system works. A friend had an eye on a particular pair of pants and a shirt for her young son. She waited for the end-of-season sale. A friendly clerk told her when that day would be. She bought her son a shirt for $2.97; it was originally marked $14.99. She bought the matching pants, originally $34.99, for only $4.97. She saved just over $42.

*Ask for discounts or rewards.* Some stores have special promotions that they call *discounts* or *rewards*. If they offer an additional 10 percent off because it is your birthday, your child's birthday, or some other occasion for a promotion, take advantage of it.

Some rewards come from in-store sales that give you a discount for using their store credit card. We don't like credit cards, but they have their place if used properly. If you can use your credit card to save the 10 percent and then head straight for the credit department to pay the charge in full, you can truly save that 10 percent. If you cannot afford the price even at the 10 percent savings, don't buy. That 10 percent could cost you much more if you end up paying over time.

*Buy seconds.* Look for seconds, blemishes, or irregulars; if these items are not discounted, ask for a discount.

*Plan ahead.* Think ahead to next season's or even next year's clothing needs. Will anyone need a new coat next winter? How about a swimming suit? Will shorts be needed to complete next summer's wardrobe? Buy at the end of one season and hold onto the item until the same season next year. If you are buying ahead for children, be sure to buy a larger size, particularly when purchasing shirts and tops. Larger shirts and tops are better and can last sometimes as long as two seasons without looking gawky.

*Use eBay.* Mothers will often box up an entire wardrobe of hand-me-downs for auction on eBay. You can buy your child's complete summer wardrobe for $5 to $20. Much of this clothing is designer brands. You can also find great bargains on Internet classifieds. In addition, you can benefit by selling the still-serviceable clothing that your own children have outgrown.

*Buy online.* Let's say you walk into a store and see an outfit you simply must have. Jot down the label and style, and look for the same item for less online

*Window-shop and bargain shop.* Window-shopping is a good way to learn prices before you go out with cash in hand.

*Use hand-me-downs.* You and your family and friends can pass on clothing that the children have outgrown. This practice cleans out your closets and allows you suitable clothing for no cost.

*Host a clothing swap.* Everyone brings the clothing they no longer want, they hang it on a rack, and they try on and select anything they want for free.

*Keep your receipts.* Place your receipts in a large envelope or file drawer for at least a month or two before tossing them out so that if you need to return something, the receipt is readily accessible.

*Invest in a sewing machine.* Sewing can be both fun and entertaining, as well as a money saver.

*Mend worn clothing.* If most of the garment still looks good, mend it. Old jeans and old pants can be cut off and made into summer shorts. Worn knees and worn seats can be replaced with patches decorated with appliques.

*Restyle basic or used clothing.* Our mothers and grandmothers were experts at cutting out new clothing—in trendy styles—from old clothing for their growing children. If elbows or knees are worn, work around them. Old clothing scraps also make beautiful quilts. Don't waste anything.

*Avoid dry-clean-only clothing for children.* Dry cleaning is expensive, and children get clothes dirty. Even grown-ups should remove dry-clean-only clothing the minute they get home and put on some wash-and-wear clothing to cut down on the expense of dry cleaning.

*Look at catalog sales.* Catalogs are fun for you and your children. We used to call them "dream" books. Latest fashions and prices for comparison shopping can be found in catalogs. But watch out! Don't be tempted to buy something just because you saw it in a catalog. You can just as easily make an impulse purchase through a catalog as you can at a store.

## Chapter 10

# Having a Really Merry Christmas

We all know the story of *How the Grinch Stole Christmas.* Theodor Geisel, known as Dr. Seuss, said he wrote the story about his own disgust with the commercialization of a holiday he loved, hoping to rediscover something about Christmas that had obviously been lost.[1]

Ted Geisel was not alone in his feelings. Christmas has become its own industry, and it's a major one. In December 2007, Americans spent $30.5 billion in the nation's department stores during the year's fourth quarter. They spent another $39 billion in Internet sales during that same quarter and $493.3 million merely on Christmas trees.[2]

Despite all the money we spend each year, what do we really remember about Christmas? We asked a few of our dearest friends and relatives to give us some answers. Their responses were surprising. Some treasured the year they had been unemployed and were forced to have a homemade Christmas. Others remembered the Christmas they never exchanged a gift but instead spent their money traveling to a disadvantaged country to build houses for the poor. One friend told us that one of her most cherished possessions is a small block of wood with a screw sticking out of it made by a grandson as a Christmas gift. Still another cherished the childhood memory of the smell of freshly baked Christmas cookies. It was interesting that no one's biggest memory was of an expensive Christmas gift they had received.

In that same spirit, here are a few ways to make your Christmas this year simpler and less expensive:

*Save ahead for Christmas gifts.* Place money in a special Christmas savings account. You can set up automatic transfers for deposits to be made weekly, monthly, or with every paycheck. If you were to put just $10 a week into a Christmas account, you would have money available for making Christmas purchases throughout the year—a total of $500 by year's end.

*Make a list and a budget.* Make a vow that you will not go into debt this Christmas. December's cheer often becomes February's headache. Before you buy, ask yourself if the person who will receive this gift really needs it. Also ask yourself how long it will take you to pay for your presents. Choose gifts wisely and keep them practical. There can be magic, even in practicality.

*Pare down your gift giving.* If this is a belt-tightening year for you, as it is for many of us, don't concern yourself with gifts for neighbors, friends, and even relatives. Slash your list of recipients by limiting Christmas gifts to just your immediate family. This will save both time and money. Or, if you really want to do something that demonstrates love, get your usual recipients together and persuade them to pool their money with yours and make a generous donation to your local food bank.

*Pool your gift money.* Go in with others, especially family members, as you would for weddings, showers, or birthdays.

*Begin the previous Christmas.* Some of our friends and family members make it a practice to buy little during the Christmas season. They actually begin their shopping with the after-Christmas sales. Clothing can be bought a year ahead for a fraction of its original price. If the clothing is for children who are still growing, just increase it one size. Continue shopping for Christmas throughout the year, and when the season rolls around, actually enjoy it!

*Shop Black Friday.* The day after Thanksgiving is a wild and crazy shopping day. The stores are filled with loss leaders. If you don't mind getting up in the middle of the night and standing in line for hours, you can often get some fabulous bargains. We particularly like to shop for electronics on Black Friday. We peruse the ads and look only for products we had planned on purchasing anyway. We've done our homework and know the make and model we want ahead of time. When we find our product in a Black Friday ad, we circle it. We try to go to only one or two places on this day, and we always plan to be home by 9 a.m. We can sometimes buy half of our Christmas presents as loss leaders. We have bought laptop computers at 60 percent off, cameras at 50 percent off, flash drives, gaming systems, and memory cards at fractions of their original price and sometimes for free with a mail-in rebate.

*Use rebates.* We often go into a store to buy something because of the lucrative rebates only to neglect to fill out the paperwork afterward. Retailers count on this. Once you get your gift home, fill out the paper work, cut off the UPC labels, and mail the rebate form immediately. Always make and keep a photocopy of your rebate paperwork in case problems should arise.

*Buy used.* Check consignment shops for clothing and games, and search the Internet before Christmas for anything from Christmas trees to yard decorations to children's toys to furniture. You can find a lot of merchandise on sale at Christmastime. Routinely check newspaper or Internet classified sites, eBay, and Craigslist. Our favorite Christmas tree came from a major department store that went out of business, and our grandchildren play with expensive toys someone practically gave away. We bought them all used.

*Scour your closets.* Do you have perfectly good books you might give away to a friend or family member, DVDs you seldom watch anymore, games or game systems that collect dust, pictures or photographs your friends or family would enjoy? You aren't a cheapskate because you give something used.

*Sell used.* To raise money for Christmas, you could also sell some of your surplus through the same avenues listed above. What you make might go toward the purchase of Christmas presents.

*White elephants.* One of our favorite practices of the year is a white elephant party with our friends. We think up wild and wacky presents all year long for just this occasion. They are generally things we have around the house, things we have inherited from our family that have no sentimental meaning, or things that just take up storage space and collect dust. We have fun passing these delightful gifts around.

*Scour the ads.* Research prices for the things you've placed on your list. When you know what you want, you can look for months and afford to wait for just the right sale. There is often a wide gap between the highest and lowest price for the same product. In addition, studying ads and scouring the Internet allows you to decide which make and model you want. Many Web sites allow you to view ratings from consumers who have already purchased the model you are looking for, and *Consumer Reports* provides you with information on the quality and options available with your particular model.

Look for loss leaders throughout the year. Don't succumb to an impulsive buy; be disciplined. Don't place yourself in the position of going to a store to buy someone a present without the foggiest idea of what you want to get and then buying the first thing you see whether they will like it or not, whether it is quality or not, and whether it is the best price or not. There is one exception to our rule. If you stumble upon an unadvertised special or a quality off-brand item at a not-to-be-beat price, you may change your mind.

*Utilize the Internet.* The Internet is a valuable tool. Not only can you purchase items online, but you can also research them for quality and price. We spend many hours online before we ever make major Christmas purchases. The Internet even has rating systems to grade specific online retailers and services. Use a service such as PayPal to protect yourself from unscrupulous retailers. If you follow these rules and use some common sense, you'll do well with Internet shopping. Also, be sure you've calculated the price of shipping into your costs.

*Discover discount and outlet stores.* Many retail chains have discount stores to sell their blemished, overstocked, and discontinued items. Don't be afraid of buying last year's model or something slightly blemished as long as it is still quality merchandise.

*Ask if there are any open-box or returned items.* Stores love to get rid of such items stored in their back rooms or warehouses. We have seen open-box computers, TVs, DVD players, cameras, and other products at fabulous prices. We have often bought these items ourselves. We still use an open-box CD, radio, and audiocassette player we bought fifteen years ago.

*Save on wrapping paper.* Wrapping paper can be homemade like anything else. Use plain paper, cutouts from old Christmas cards, stamps, paints, or children's crayon drawings to decorate. If this seems like too much work, how about "naked" presents? We all remember those days from our childhood when unwrapped presents were placed lovingly under the tree and gobbled up by starry-eyed youngsters.

We have friends who save used wrapping paper for reuse next season and others who only buy wrapping paper at after-Christmas sales and save it for the following year. Wrapping paper need not be expensive.

*Make homemade gifts.* Often, the most treasured gifts are made by the creative hands of a friend or family member. Framed family photographs, paintings, crafts, needlework, quilts, scrapbook pages, and warm holiday treats are always welcome gifts.

While you are at it, make your own Christmas cards or make Christmas cards for friends and family as their Christmas gift. Make Christmas wreaths from the boughs you cut from the bottom of your tree or from scraps at a Christmas tree lot you can pick up for a song.

String popcorn and cranberries, make paper chains and advent calendars, drizzle glue and glitter on pinecones, or make a mix of your favorite cookie recipe or the fixings for a soup. There is no end of creative gifts to give to those you love.

*Remember the needy.* Sponsor a child through charity. Do your own Sub-for-Santa. Collect coats, gloves, scarves, and hats for a rescue mission. Put together hygiene kits to give to a humanitarian center. Raise money for a charity with your neighbors instead of exchanging gifts with them. Give to those who really need a Christmas.

*File all your receipts.* As soon as you begin to buy presents for Christmas, file away the receipts for exchanges. We keep a big manila envelope next to our mail. It is open and accessible. It allows us to never lose a critical receipt and to find receipts when we need to make returns.

After Christmas, empty your receipt envelope, staple the receipts to the warranties, and file them again. Now you are prepared should you ever need to use your warranty. We have been grateful on many occasions for this system.

*Don't neglect the things that cost nothing.* Spend an hour caroling with your family, read Christmas stories around the fire, and share your favorite scripture verses about the Savior, including the precious words from Luke. None of this will cost you a dime. When the love of the Lord fills our hearts, we give as He did.

# Chapter 11

# Good Health Is like Cash in the Bank

"To keep our body in good health is a duty," said Gautama Siddharta, better known as Buddha. "Otherwise we shall not be able to keep our mind strong and clear."[1] That is sage advice. But keeping healthy also saves us money. This chapter is divided into three sections: insurance tips, prevention tips, and services tips.

## Insurance Tips

*Carry medical insurance.* The greatest savings and security against high medical bills is to carry medical insurance. When shopping for a healthcare plan, don't select one simply because it offers the lowest monthly premium or because it was one you used before. Rather, investigate your health insurance as carefully as you investigate a potential home or car—maybe even more carefully because your life could depend on it.

There are many different types of medical insurance plans. There are HMOs, PPOs, and managed-care plans. Benefits for whatever plan you choose are likely to vary year to year, so keep current with the latest policy benefits. If you are employed by a company that offers medical insurance, read through current plan coverage every year during open enrollment. Assess your family's health and economic condition before deciding which plan best suits your needs.

*Bargain shop.* Jot down your family's average number of yearly visits to the doctor and the dentist, and examine your current prescription record. If your medical insurance company has a Web site, at the end of the year print out all of your doctor visits and a list of your pharmaceuticals and their costs. Compare and contrast your actual needs with the differing plan options, and don't forget to take into consideration monthly premiums and deductibles.

*Consider a high deductible.* If the cost of insurance premiums is eating you alive, you can save hundreds of dollars a year in lower premiums by simply opting for a higher deductible. The way that many high-deductible plans work is that your insurance will not pay any benefits until your costs have exceeded an established threshold, such as $1,100 for individuals or $2,200 for families. If your family members are healthy and seldom go to the doctor, this is a fabulous option.

Some high-deductible plans offer an additional health-savings account. This is a special pretax account that will pay your insurance premiums and your out-of-pocket expenses below the threshold. However, if your family has chronic and costly health conditions, if you are not disciplined about depositing money into a health-savings account, or if the high deductible makes you uneasy, opt for a more traditional plan.

*Farm Bureau, AARP, health co-ops.* Such organizations offer savings on your health insurance. You do not even need to be a farmer to join your state's farm bureau. By paying a modest annual membership fee, you are eligible to receive discounted group health insurance. Group health co-ops are available and offer individual and family plans with lower rates and greater physician choices. When you are self-employed, at or near retirement, or in some other similar circumstance, you will benefit by exploring all these avenues for lower health care premiums.

*Dental plans.* Dental plans are also offered through special discount clubs. Availability, rates, and the names of these plans can be found on the Internet. Participating dentists agree to give members of these discount clubs up to 60 percent savings on their bill in exchange for a monthly membership fee. However, you will probably need to pay cash at the time of service.

*Sign up for FSA.* Flexible spending accounts are tax-sheltered accounts that reimburse out-of-pocket payments on medical expenses, including doctors' visits, hospitalization and surgery, medical tests, eyeglasses, prescriptions, and sometimes over-the-counter medications. To enroll, estimate the cost of your annual medical expenses for the next year and subtract about 20 percent. You cannot recoup any excess FSA funds, so you do not want to go under your allotment. However, when you find yourself under your FSA withholding with the year drawing to an end, find ways to spend your withholding by buying new glasses or contacts, having your teeth cleaned, or purchasing over-the-counter medications and bandages.

*Take advantage of other perks in your plan.* Visit your insurance company's Web site to learn of extra advantages offered. Does your insurance company have nurses on call to answer medical questions? Does it have advisory services to help manage a medical condition such as asthma or heart disease? Does it offer discounts on gym memberships, massage treatments, or weight-loss programs? Take advantage of any perks that meet the needs of your family, especially if they save you money.

*Don't take no for an answer.* If your insurance company refuses to pay for a service you think you deserve, appeal it. If you are denied a second time, contact your state's insurance commission to mediate. Negotiations take time, sometimes months, but they are worth trying.

*Take a list of your insurance company's "formulary" medicines to your doctor.* To save on rising prescription costs, consult your insurance company's covered prescription medications and ask your doctor if he can prescribe from your company's formulary list. In addition, if your insurer requires that you see a specialist from a preferred-provider list, consult with your primary-care physician about those on the list.

*Are you short on cash?* Don't be embarrassed to tell your doctor or dentist if you are in tight financial circumstances. Most physicians will suggest less costly options, and some will offer you prescription samples to help you through the tough times.

*Can you cut your pills in half?* Sometimes high-dose medications are less costly than lower-dose equivalents when cut in half. In other words, if your dosage is 25 mg, and a 50 mg pill is less expensive than two smaller-dosage pills, ask your doctor to prescribe the 50-mg pill and set the dosage instructions to one-half pill per day. Then simply cut the big pill into two. Caution! This option does not work for timed-release medications.

*Read your bills and explanation-of-benefits statements.* Make sure there are no errors in your benefits or charges. Your insurance company will appreciate it if you spot an error in the statement of services, and your doctor will appreciate it if you find that the insurance company actually owes more than it paid him. Mostly, errors are to your benefit. You are responsible for making sure that you are billed correctly. Know that not all your bills will be accurate.

*What if you lose your insurance?* Since 1985 temporary insurance has been made available to those who lose their benefits temporarily, generally due to unemployment. This type of coverage is known as COBRA. The provisions of the law are complicated, but COBRA allows employees and their families to briefly extend their current health benefits while looking for new employment or waiting for new coverage to begin. Mail-in prescription benefits are also offered through COBRA.

COBRA coverage is expensive and can be a shock to the unemployed. Here is the situation in a nutshell. Unemployed individuals received an average of $1,278 per month in 2008 through state managed-unemployment assistance programs, but individual health insurance through COBRA requires almost 30 percent of the unemployment assistance paycheck while insurance for a family eats up 80 percent.[2] No wonder only 9 percent of laid-off workers take advantage of COBRA coverage, though 66 percent of laid-off workers are eligible. The average health care premiums under COBRA can total $4,704 per year per individual and $12,680 per family. In addition, 38 percent of laid-off workers are at a particular disadvantage because they worked for companies or individuals who offered them no insurance coverage to begin with.[3]

There are other options. Medical insurance for the unemployed is available through online insurance or through local agents. Only reputable Web sites or companies should be used under this option. The same advice we have offered previously applies. Ask government agencies, experts, medical doctors, and the Better Business Bureau before you buy anything.

Forty states provide insurance coverage for the unemployed through continuation insurance that is similar to COBRA but extended to companies who employ fewer than twenty workers. Check with your state government to see if this is a good option for you.

Some policyholders can convert their benefits. Lisa Nichols, writing for www.suite101.com, says, "Insurance group health plans that offer conversions may allow a policyholder to convert unemployment group health benefits to an individual insurance policy."[4] She suggests that many people are also eligible for job loss insurance through the Health Insurance Portability and Accountability Act of 1996. "Unemployed people who are eligible for HIPAA are guaranteed two health insurance policy offers."[5]

Check with your state insurance department to find out HIPAA eligibility requirements. Low-income individuals may be eligible for insurance through Medicaid, and high-risk pools offer health insurance for the unemployed, though these high-risk pools are costly.

Prescription assistance may also be available as an unemployed health benefit through a pharmaceutical company. This assistance provides those without insurance the benefit of meeting prescription costs. Local pharmacies know the different discount drug plan benefits or other benefits available to the unemployed. When in doubt, talk to your pharmacist, and don't neglect to ask about generics. Switching from a name brand to a generic alternative can often lower your prescription costs without reducing quality. We'll discuss more about generic medication later. Consult your doctor before making the switch.

In addition, for healthy individuals and families, short-term insurance is also available. It can be an option to COBRA. Short-term insurance is generally more cost-effective as temporary insurance because such policies are not written annually but rather month to month. They cover major medical expenses, including inpatient and outpatient care. They are up to 70 percent less expensive than COBRA, and policyholders are free to choose any doctor or hospital. The disadvantage of short-term insurance is that it will not cover preexisting conditions. Plans may be compared online at www.ehealthinsurance.com.

State legislatures and the U.S. Congress are grappling with other options for the relief of those who find themselves temporarily unemployed. Check with the government for the latest options available.

# Prevention

*Be prudent.* Learn the laws of health and obey them. Do not neglect annual physical examinations even when you do not feel sick. Caught in the early stages, even serious illnesses can be quickly cured or managed. Establish a regular exercise program to help your family stave off disease or to manage the ill effects of having one. Walking is less expensive and probably the most beneficial health program you can adopt. In addition to walking, there are other inexpensive forms of exercise such as swimming, aerobics, jogging, and bicycling.

Never jump right into exercise. Warm up slowly to avoid strains and pain. Spend five minutes in a low-intensity workout.

Stretch your muscles and then go for high-intensity aerobic exercises that raise your heart rate and blood pressure. Exercise boosts your energy, tones your body, improves your heart and lung health, strengthens your bones, lowers your LDL (bad cholesterol), and raises your HDL (good cholesterol). It also lowers your risk for type 2 diabetes, heart disease, and certain types of cancer.

*Don't buy expensive gym memberships.* If you must have a gym membership, check with your county's recreation department for memberships, or buy your own gym equipment. Used gym equipment is plentiful and inexpensive. Many people buy equipment but then allow it to collect dust after their fitness impulse wanes. Ask around your circle of friends and family to see if anyone has any equipment they no longer use. Check Internet sites for used equipment. Once you have found what you want, offer less than the asking price or offer to barter. Sometimes you can get equipment for free if the owner needs the space more than he wants the money.

*Eat healthfully.* Eat five to eight servings of fruits and vegetables a day, especially fresh varieties. Avoid processed food, and opt for higher fiber and lower calories. Limit your eating out, keep fat grams to a minimum, and watch your portions. Meat portions should be no larger than a deck of cards, and pasta and rice portions should be kept to the size of a tennis ball. Eating healthfully is likewise critical to dental health. We tend to think of sugar as detrimental to our teeth, but it is actually a combination of starches and sugar that is the real culprit. Imagine sugar and glue, and you'll get the idea.

*Brush your teeth.* Keeping your teeth brushed and flossed may not only improve dental health and eliminate costly trips to the dentist but also may improve your heart's health.

*Wash your hands.* We spend a lot of money every year on remedies for colds and flu. Washing your hands more frequently might eliminate much cost. Teach your children to scrub their hands at least twenty seconds before eating, after playing outside, or after being around someone who is sick.

*Get regular dental checkups.* Children should begin seeing a dentist twice a year after their first birthday (provided they have teeth).

*Wear helmets.* Don't let your children ride a bike, scooter, or skateboard without a helmet.

*Wear good shoes.* Many injuries can be prevented by wearing good, supportive shoes.

# Services

*Ask for a second opinion.* If a test or procedure sounds expensive and you're not sure it is necessary, ask for a second opinion. If your physician advises surgery, ask another physician for an assessment.

*Don't go to the emergency room unless it is a real emergency.* Because of the cost, going to the emergency room is no substitute for a visit to a doctor's office.

*Go generic.* Tell your pharmacist that generic substitutions for your prescriptions are all right. Only rarely are brand names better quality than their generic counterpart. Also, some discount stores and pharmacies now offer generic medication for $4 for a month's supply and $10 for a ninety-day supply.

*Save money on eye glasses and contact lenses.* Eye glasses and contact lenses do not have to be bought from an optometrist or an ophthalmologist. You can take a copy of your prescription to the provider of your choice. You can look at discount stores and even online for providers offering the identical prescription with the same quality product and even brand name as the more expensive provider associated with your doctor's office.

*Opt for dental schools.* If you live near a dental school, you can opt for service from student dentists. You'll be charged 20 to 50 percent less, which is a huge savings when it comes to crowns or implants.

Chapter 12

# The Benefits and Pitfalls of Insurance

Insurance can be one of the least understood and most confusing pieces in a family's financial puzzle, and yet, who among us can afford to live without it? Do we have too much? Too little? What kind of insurance policies will benefit us most? How do we shop for a trusted company and a caring agent? We will attempt to answer these questions in this chapter.

President N. Eldon Tanner, who was a member of the First Presidency, advised: "Nothing seems so certain as the unexpected in our lives. . . . Every family should make provision for proper health and life insurance."[1] One of the surest ways to financial ruin is to make no provisions for insurance that can see us safely through the storms of life.

Merriam-Webster's online dictionary defines insurance as "coverage by contract whereby one party undertakes to indemnify or guarantee against loss by a specified contingency or peril."[2] There are differing forms and types of insurance and countless numbers of companies. So many types of insurance are available that to give advice on all of them would be dizzying. We will offer in this chapter some general rules that cover many forms of insurance and some savings tips for general categories.

# General Insurance Strategies

*Buy the broadest coverage possible.* Instead of flight insurance, cancer insurance, or accidental death insurance, look into a good broad plan. Health insurance that covers cancer is better than cancer insurance. A life insurance policy ought to cover your family no matter how you die, whether from an accident at home or in an airplane crash.

*Shop, shop, shop.* Shopping takes time, but it pays great dividends. Talk to your friends and associates, visit the Yellow Pages, call your state insurance department (you'll find the phone number online or in the phone book with the government agencies), and consult the Better Business Bureau. Always buy from licensed, highly rated companies with proven track records. Once you receive a quote from a company, take the quote to the Internet to make comparisons. A good, reliable consumer organization that can provide you with much-needed information is the National Association of Insurance Commissioners (www.naic.org). A review of the NAIC Web site is most informative. You can research individual insurers by state, and you can review complaints. In addition, the site contains press releases, consumer alerts, audits, reports, and avenues for registering complaints.

The National Insurance Consumer Organization, or the Consumer Federation of America, also provides much-needed information for your comparison shopping. Internet searches can provide you with countless similar organizations and allow you to shop extensively from the privacy of your home.

In our volatile market, the wise consumer must also consult the financial stability of competing insurance providers. Rating companies such as A. M. Best (www.ambest.com) and Standard & Poor's (www.standardandpoors.com) can assist you in this quest. Before buying anything, narrow your field to at least three insurers, get price quotes, and assess the reliability of your potential agent.

*Raise your deductible.* A deductible is the amount of money you must pay as part of an insurance claim. The higher your deductible, the lower your premium. Most insurance companies recommend at least a $500 deductible, but if you can afford to raise it to $1,000, you will save 25 percent in annual premiums.

With automobile insurance there may be one deductible for automobile damage and another for personal injury. In areas prone to hurricanes, floods, tornadoes, and so forth, your insurance may have a separate deductible for each sort of disaster damage. For example, those who reside in the eastern United States may have one deductible for wind damage and another for hail.

*Don't overinsure or underinsure.* Adequate coverage will vary depending on the form of insurance you purchase. We'll discuss coverages later. As a governing principle, just be sure you are not paying high premiums for coverage you don't need.

*Look for discounts.* Does your bank or credit union or employer offer discounts with a particular provider? Are you retired? Are you in excellent health? Are you a nonsmoker? Do you belong to a professional association? Most companies offer some sort of discounts on insurance.

*Stay with the same insurer.* Once you have found a policy, a company, and an agent you like, stay with them as long as possible. After having been with a company for many years, you may receive special discounts for being a long-term policyholder. Some insurers will reduce your premiums by 5 percent for staying with them as little as three to five years and 10 percent for being with them for six or more years. In addition, some companies will give you a preferred discount if you go to them for all of your insurance needs. However, there may be occasions when a change of provider is warranted. Be wise and be flexible.

*Price is not the only consideration.* The reliability of your company and your agent ought to influence your decision as much as the price of the premium. Many companies are notorious for taking forever to pay; others cancel you abruptly for making one small claim. Good agents will call you if they feel that you can save money on your insurance, if levels of insurance are likely to go up or down, or if specialized policies come along that they think you might be interested in. Good agents and reliable companies are worth their weight in gold.

# Types and Forms of Insurance

Anything can be insured, and in today's world almost everything has its own kind of insurance. Insurance, however, can be broken into four general categories: home, auto, life and disability, and health. We covered health insurance in a previous chapter; in this chapter we will explore home, auto, and life and disability.

### Home Insurance

Home insurance, as well as auto insurance, provides protection for property and against casualty. Property insurance protects you from losses sustained by damage to or destruction of some real, tangible asset. Generally, home insurance policies carry exclusions and exceptions, which are generally included in the policy statement. Exclusions include but are not limited to rodent damage, intentional or negligent acts of destruction, motor vehicle and watercraft liability, or business and rental property. Some natural disasters are excluded from coverage. These exclusions often include floods, hurricanes, volcanoes, and earthquakes. To receive coverage for these disasters often requires additional insurance policies.

Whether you need disaster insurance depends entirely upon the risk level of your area. If your home is located within a "hundred-year floodplain"—meaning that a flood has occurred somewhere on your land within the past hundred years—you ought to invest in flood insurance. On the other hand, if recent high claims have inflicted severe damage to your insurance company's financial health, the company may discontinue specialized insurance for certain disasters in an entire area. Such an example can be found in the southern United States, where such enormous claims were paid to victims of Hurricane Katrina that companies faced virtual bankruptcy. In some of these states, hurricane insurance is no longer available.

Finding specialized policies to cover flood, wind, and earthquake damage can be easy. You can find resources through the Federal Emergency Management Agency Web site. Search Web sites or call your state insurance department to find companies and policies offered in your state.

*Casualty insurance.* Casualty protects you from any act that causes personal injury or death as well as from harm or injury to another person's property. Liability insurance is a form of casualty insurance.

*Liability coverage.* Insuring for *legal fees* can also be included within the casualty clauses of your homeowner's insurance. In today's litigious society it is almost a necessity to carry protection against enormous legal fees. Because so many people sue and because awards are often large, liability insurance is often expensive. There are exclusions to liability coverage in the same way as there are exclusions to property coverage.

*Replacement coverage.* It is not only necessary to have coverage for the value of your home and property, but it is also necessary that you have *full-replacement coverage* for the value for your assets. Replacement value means you can rebuild your home and replace its contents to its current condition and not some former condition. You will be offered actual replacement costs, regardless of your home's age, or you will be offered coverage for the actual value of your home and possessions, less an amount for the age of the home.

*Review your policy and the value of your possessions on a routine basis.* It is a good idea to have your home and rebuilding costs reevaluated every two to three years. Remember that your home value includes the land, whereas rebuilding costs include only the cost of the structures on your property.

*Prepare written and photographic documentation of your home and property.* Inventory and record your possessions, and record make, model, and serial numbers of expensive possessions like computers, televisions, and major appliances. Photograph everything on your premises, including jewelry and coin collections. Store your written inventories and photographs in a safe place away from your home where they will be safe in the event of an emergency. Keep major-purchase sales slips, warranties, and similar documents in a metal file cabinet to protect them against fire and flood. These written and photographic documents will provide vital information for your insurance company in the event that you make a claim.

*Renter's insurance.* If you do not own your home, you can obtain renter's insurance to protect your possessions from theft and disaster.

*Home security.* Discounts are offered for additions like smoke detectors, burglar alarms, and deadbolts. Some companies will cut your premiums by as much as 15 to 20 percent if you install automatic sprinkler systems. Such systems are expensive and not cost effective unless you have a large home. Talk to your agent frequently, and ask if there are other safety additions for which you might be given a discount to your policy.

*Make your home resistant to disaster.* Take whatever steps you can to keep your home safe from fires, windstorms, and other disasters. Add storm shutters if you live in high-wind areas. Reinforce your roof or buy stronger roofing materials if necessary. Older homes can be retrofitted to be more earthquake resistant. Modernize your heating, plumbing, and electrical to bring them up to new building codes.

*Maintain a good credit rating.* Solid credit can cut your insurance costs. Insurers share credit information when offering you a quote on a homeowner's policy. Pay your bills on time, and keep credit balances low. Check your credit rating on a routine basis for errors.

*Buy and maintain auto and homeowner's insurance policies from the same company.* Some companies offer as much as a 5 to 15 percent savings for having both policies from them.

## Auto Insurance

If you own an automobile, your state will undoubtedly require that you carry automobile insurance. A basic auto insurance policy covers you and your vehicle against property damage caused by you or others, bodily injury caused by you or others, and medical costs arising from injuries received by you or others. It also covers collision damage sustained by your car or caused by your car to another car or to someone else's property. Comprehensive coverage covers damage caused by rocks, hail, fire, theft, and sometimes uninsured drivers. (In some states, insurance for uninsured drivers is a separate add-on.) Check with your state insurance department for a publication of typical prices charged by different companies operating in your area.

*Know your exclusions.* Read through your policy carefully, and know what is excluded from your policy's coverage. Obtain the proper amount of coverage, and avoid high premiums that might be better invested in a savings account for emergencies.

*Avoid vehicles that are expensive to insure.* Before purchasing a car, call your agent to see if the new car you are considering falls into this category. Some cars are poor safety risks, and others are poor property risks. Avoid them both.

*Ask for discounts.* Does your company offer good-student rates? Nonsmoker rates? Safe-driver rates? Is there a discount for having both your auto and homeowner's insurance policies through your company? Does your credit union or bank offer discounts by buying insurance through certain companies?

*Consider the age of your vehicle.* If your vehicle is putting on the years, consider dropping all but liability insurance on it. Collision, towing, and windshield coverage may not be worth the expense once your car has reached a certain age. There is one exception to this rule: Keep your comprehensive coverage if you live in a high-crime area where there is high incidence of theft and vandalism.

*Making claims against an auto or homeowner's insurance policy.* Do not make frivolous claims. If the amount of damage sustained is at least twice the cost of your deductible, it is worth filing a claim. However, if you make too many claims within a certain number of years, generally three, your policy may be canceled. In addition, each claim you make will increase the amount of your premium.

When making a claim, support it with photographic evidence of the damage. Your company may do its own photos, but it doesn't hurt to keep your own photographic record.

*Shop again periodically.* Run a check on premium prices now and again to make sure you are still getting the best deal. Don't cancel a policy until you have a new one, however, and investigate the claim-and-cancellation record of a prospective company and the reliability of a prospective agent.

## Life and Disability Insurance

Life insurance is an absolute necessity. Your life is worth a specific dollar amount based upon your earning power and your importance to your loved ones. There are two basic types of life insurance, *cash-value life* and *term life.* Cash-value insurance, also known as whole, universal, or variable depending upon the policy, is designed to offer a built-in savings plan. The insurance company agrees to pay interest on the extra money you pay in premiums. This cash value is always yours, and the theory is that you can borrow against it in the event you need it. However, it can cost as much as eight times, or 800 percent "more than comparable term policies," says Eric Tyson, MBA and author of *Personal Finance for Dummies.*[3]

If you haven't had your policy very long and you wish to borrow against it, you may have to pay a surrender charge to free your cash value, which is a percentage of what you have paid in premiums. In other words, you may have to pay more of your own money to take out your own money. Cash value does not accrue much, if at all, in the first year or two of your policy anyway.

Most insurance experts will probably discourage you from purchasing a whole-life policy. Whole life is an investment insurance, but in most cases investments can be better made elsewhere (depending, of course, on the economic climate and the specific policy). Whole-life policies cost a lot of money.

Term life policies are generally less expensive and a better value over the long run. They are offered through your employer and from private companies. Policies offered through your employer are usually offered at a significant discount and are available as long as you are employed by that company. Their cost, however, rises with your age.

Private term insurance eventually reaches its term limit—ten to thirty years. When you get older, maintaining your private policy will cost you much more. Ten-year rates will obviously be much lower than thirty-year rates. But once you reach a certain age, the need for your policy will decrease because your children will move out of your care and your mortgage will be paid.

*How much coverage do I need?* You can estimate that amount by multiplying your gross income by 80 percent if you are a low-income earner, by 70 percent if you are a middle-income earner, or by 60 percent if you are a high-income earner. Also, you may want to include in your estimate the age of your children, the cost of college education, and the price of your mortgage before you determine an amount. You can find useful insurance calculators at moneycentral.msn.com and smartmoney.com.

*What about life insurance for a stay-at-home spouse?* A stay-at-home spouse contributes to the family's net worth by the value his or her service brings to the family. If, for example, your stay-at-home spouse were to die, you might need to pay for child care and housekeeping services. A life insurance policy could offset that cost.

*What about life insurance for children?* Some experts advise that you not get a life insurance policy for your children because most children outlive their parents, and the price of the premium is not worth the benefit. We did take out such policies, but we only bought coverage to cover funeral expenses. Children's policies offered through your employer are usually limited and inexpensive. Look at the cost and determine your need.

*Should I purchase accident insurance or disability insurance?* Obviously, if your employer offers accident coverage with your benefits package, you would be foolish to opt out, but if you aren't offered any, don't buy. Your life is as valuable to your survivors whether you die from a heart attack or in an accident. There is no appreciable benefit from an accident insurance policy.

On the other hand, disability insurance is sound and cost-effective. There is far more likelihood that you will become disabled than that you will die. The ability to bring home a paycheck is more valuable than anything else. The most important policy you might buy is a disability policy. Many employers not only offer disability insurance but pay the premiums for you as well. If you don't know whether you have such a policy, find out. If you don't have one, consider getting one.

*Mortgage insurance.* We have already covered mortgage insurance in a previous chapter. Once you owe less than 80 percent of the value of your home, you no longer need mortgage insurance. Generally, mortgage insurance is of such poor value that you would be better to simply factor the value of your mortgage into your life insurance coverage.

*Travel insurance.* This is generally a waste of money and is based upon the same principles articulated in our discussion of accident insurance. However, if you purchase plane tickets using certain credit cards, you will find that you automatically receive travel insurance.

*Other forms of life insurance.* What about universal, variable, and other types of insurance? For advice on other types of insurance, talk to a professional—someone you can trust and who will give you sound advice. Never fall for the hard sales pitch. Keep a cool head, and do your homework before making any decisions. If you make a mistake with the purchase of a policy, cancel it and chalk up your mistake to experience. Nothing is set in stone. Your needs and financial situation change, and you must do what is best for you and your family.

# PART THREE

# Surviving Tough Times

# Chapter 13

# The Difference between Ants and Grasshoppers

It is always difficult to give someone else advice on savings, particularly when you are not an expert. On the other hand, it is difficult to comprehend the advice of experts, as there are so many opinions. Will Rogers offered perhaps the soundest advice: "Don't gamble. Take all your savings and buy some good stock and hold it till it goes up. Then sell it. If it don't go up, don't buy it."[1]

## Save for the Necessities of Life

Probably the best advice we can offer is to save a portion of your income. This has long been the advice of sages. Consider the fable of the ant and the grasshopper:

In a field one summer's day a Grasshopper was hopping about, chirping and singing to its heart's content. An Ant passed by, bearing along with great toil an ear of corn he was taking to the nest.

"Why not come and chat with me," said the Grasshopper, "instead of toiling and moiling in that way?"

"I am helping to lay up food for the winter," said the Ant, "and recommend you to do the same."

"Why bother about winter?" said the Grasshopper. "We have got plenty of food at present."

But the Ant went on its way and continued its toil. When the winter came the Grasshopper had no food and found itself dying of hunger while it saw the ants distributing every day corn and grain from the stores they had collected in the summer. Then the Grasshopper knew: "IT IS BEST TO PREPARE FOR THE DAYS OF NECESSITY."[2]

The fable, credited to a Greek slave who lived 620–540 B.C., was built upon the wisdom of saving that is as sound today as it was two and a half millennia ago. What we save, how much we save, and where we put our money is a matter of personal preference. But Church leaders have encouraged us to save for a day of necessity.

Failing to contribute to an employee incentive savings program is foolish for at least a couple of reasons. First, we miss out on the employer match many businesses offer. Second, most of us possess neither the discipline nor the expertise to invest our money ourselves. How much you contribute has to be based on your circumstances. Consider that it is always wise to set aside money first for emergencies and then for such future needs as education. Retirement and fulfillment of personal dreams are worth saving for.

Putting money aside offers you control of your future, your security, and your standard of living. The road to personal wealth is built while you are eliminating your debt, though you will want to be more aggressive once you are free from financial bondage. Money cannot buy happiness, but it can provide security.

Can security really be achieved in a world where retirement savings have taken enormous hits? The answer is yes. Every method of savings has some risk. How aggressively you invest depends on the level of risk with which you are comfortable. Some enjoy conservative savings; they like the security of a passbook savings account. Others are lured by the larger earnings that come from the bond or stock markets.

Whatever you do, employ the services of a trusted and reliable financial adviser. Finding someone who is always 100 percent right will be impossible, but finding someone who is honest, with a proven track record, who pays attention to your needs is doable. Remember that you can always switch financial advisers if the need arises. Your responsibility is to your family and their needs. Keep your money safe.

# Save What Is Sufficient for Your Needs

The key to saving is simply to save sufficient for our needs. What is sufficient? It is an amount decided upon by two equal partners in marriage in counsel with the Lord. The Church has already advised us to store a supply of food, clothing, and, where possible, fuel. In addition, Church leadership advises that we keep a cash reserve of three months in case of emergencies.

Happiness exceeds the size of a bank account. If you build your life around how much money and how many goods you've accumulated, you will find that your spiritual bank account is empty. Often we forget some of life's most important lessons. President Spencer W. Kimball taught these:

> What honor is there in being the richest man in the cemetery?

> We live in a corrupt world where most of the things we *think* we want can be purchased with money or obtained through political power, but we also live in a wonderfully good world where the things which really bring us unbounded joy may still be had in rich abundance if we are willing to pay the price, and that price is expressed not in money but in effort.

This nation thought it had found the abundant life in 1929 when luxury came alike to the lowly and the well-to-do, greater luxury than that enjoyed by early kings and emperors. We were driving our unpaid-for autos over heavily bonded highways, en route to the bank to make the monthly installment payments on the radio, the refrigerator, the vacuum cleaner, on Father's new golf clubs and on Mother's new gown. Luxury-mad, we were borrowing from and bonding the generations yet unborn that we might have an abundance of the things which gave comfort, pleasure, and ease. Did this increase our joy? Not at all. This was a poor substitute for the abundant life. Crime increased, divorces were more usual, homes were broken up. Finally, the end came to this orgy of spending. The Depression followed . . . but after the smoke had cleared away, we found attendance at church services increased, friendships assumed new value, fellowship of interests was the rule, and men began to appreciate each other and again live a fuller life. For again rang down through the centuries the words of Divinity: 'For a man's life consisteth not in the abundance of the things which he possesseth. . . . The life is more than meat, and the body is more than raiment . . . but seek ye first the kingdom of God and its righteousness, and all other things will be added unto you.' (See Luke 12:15–31.)

Having lost their expensive cars, or unable to purchase gasoline for them, groups remained at home and found real joy in family associations and in teaching the children the way of life. Short of means to lavish on expensive and showy parties, neighbors were content to visit in true friendship. Without means to sustain the club or social group, men and women again found good books interesting and companionable. And life again took on a new meaning.[3]

We face similar challenges in our own day. We forget that we must keep in perspective the blessings that the Lord continues to shower upon us. We must be in the world but not of the world. If we adopt the world's view that *sufficient* means having more than our neighbor, we do not understand what God wants.

Let's go back to the idyllic setting recorded in the Book of Mormon: "And they had all things common among them; therefore there were not *rich and poor,* bond and free, but they were all made free, and partakers of the heavenly gift" (4 Nephi 1:3; emphasis added). The concept of neither rich nor poor was such a superlative state that the scriptural account reports that "there could not be a happier people among all the people who had been created by the hand of God" (4 Nephi 1:16).

# Other Savings That Will Fill Our Eternal Bank Accounts

President Kimball again warns:

Many people spend most of their time working in the service of a self-image that includes sufficient money, stocks, bonds, investment portfolios, property, credit cards, furnishings, automobiles, and the like to *guarantee* carnal security throughout, it is hoped, a long and happy life. Forgotten is the fact that our assignment is to use these many resources in our families and quorums to build up the kingdom of God—to further the missionary effort and the genealogical and temple work; to raise our children up as fruitful servants unto the Lord; to bless others in every way, that they may also be fruitful. Instead, we expend these blessings on our own desires, and as Moroni said, "Ye adorn yourselves with that which hath no life, and yet suffer the hungry, and the needy, and the naked, and the sick and the afflicted to pass by you, and notice them not." (Mormon 8:39.)[4]

In conclusion, save, save, save! Save not for riches but with wisdom; save for the needs of your family and the relief of the needy. Follow the direction of Paul:

"Charge them that are rich in this world, that they be not high-minded, nor trust in uncertain riches, but in the living God, who giveth us richly all things to enjoy; that they do good, that they be rich in good works, ready to distribute, willing to communicate; laying up in store for themselves a good foundation against the time to come, that they may lay hold on eternal life" (1 Timothy 6:17–19).

# Chapter 14

# Starving the Beast

Bertrand Russell said, "It is preoccupation with possessions, more than anything else, that prevents men from living freely and nobly."[1] The prophet Mormon addressed materialism many centuries ago: "Behold, I speak unto you as if ye were present, and yet ye are not. But behold, Jesus Christ hath shown you unto me, and I know your doing. . . . For behold, ye do love money, and your substance, and your fine apparel, and the adorning of your churches [and your houses], more than ye love the poor and the needy, the sick and the afflicted" (Mormon 8:35–37).

We have recently met so many who feel that they have been thrust into desperate circumstances. The fragile economy has exposed the breadth and depth of their financial peril. They are part of a large and growing group of people who are feeling trapped and frightened and who face a growing mountain of debt. They have lost all sense of security and now stare into the gaping jaws of a hungry financial beast.

How could so many of us have fallen prey to this beast? It's simple, really: we have been led down a seductive path. We have participated in a culture for which spending is the norm. Even our political leaders urge us to spend: "Spend for the good of the country! Use our stimulus money to pay down your debts! Don't hoard it by putting it into savings!"

For decades we could not turn on the TV, tune in to the radio, or pick up the mail without being enticed by yet another credit card offer. We couldn't speak to a friend without our conversation turning to a discussion of the latest fashion, the most coveted automobile, or our longing for some new item of home furnishing. Even if we somehow resisted all these temptations, even if we were not spending beyond our means, we were not entirely immune to the pain caused by this debt-ridden monster because we always knew someone who was not able to escape it. Nearly all of society had become the beast's slaves, and we all lived in fear that unless we kept the beast fed and happy, he would turn and devour us.

The media has been awash with stories about outrageous indiscretions by corporate bosses, financiers, and Wall Street tycoons. We are aghast at their follies, but in reality we have all played a part in this era of self-indulgence that has recently come crashing down upon us.

Are you aware that currently consumer debt in the United States now stands at $2.57 trillion, and do you know that it rises exponentially every year? In 2006 it was $2.39 trillion, but in 2007 it was $2.46 trillion. At the zenith of our economic bubble in 2008, the Federal Reserve reported that we were spending 14.3 percent of our after-tax income servicing our debts. Is it any wonder that almost half of American families—43 percent—spend more than they earn each year?

Servitude to the beast is so embarrassing that most of its victims suffer in silence. From all outward appearances, these victims have no real financial problems. They pay their bills on time and look affluent. In fact, only recently have they even realized they were in any danger. Their bondage came upon them so slowly and so imperceptibly that only a sudden reversal of fortune revealed their plight. Now they are surprised and ashamed.

Contrary to current popular belief, we will never be free of this beast by simply throwing money at it. We can't get out of a debt morass by spending more, and we can't change society's dynamic by printing more money and using even more credit. We must engage this beast in battle and cut off its food supply. This beast is slain only through starvation.

Jay MacDonald at Bankrate.com observes: "Studies estimate that as many as 17 million Americans, better than one in 20 of us, can't control our urge to shop, even at the expense of our job, our marriage, our family and our finances."[2]

This has happened because we live in a shop-happy society. For years we made jokes about it, and we laughed at the fact that many of us had succumbed to a "shop-till-you-drop" mentality. But for a true shopaholic, it is no laughing matter. It is a compulsive disorder which destroys peace of mind, family harmony, and interpersonal relationships.

> There are chemical messengers known as neurotransmitters that carry communication from your brain to . . . your body. When you're anxious, nervous, or feeling worried (like when self-critical thoughts start creeping in), you get a flood of panic-inducing epinephrine that can feel like pure jet fuel. When something happens that makes you feel especially good (like when you buy something!), you get a rush of incredibly satisfying neurotransmitters called serotonins that feels GREAT.
>
> Spending addiction causes "I've got to buy something NOW" behavior. Each "cha-ching!" of the cash register or credit card "Approved!" message makes you feel so good, you get enough of a chemical rush to drown in. One purchase is never enough. You want to feel that exhilarating "high" again and again and again—and keep those nagging, distressing feelings at arm's length. And so you go out and buy something.
>
> You've become intoxicated by your own behavior. The only thing that feels important is to be able to continue spending—because shopping for and acquiring

new things makes you feel so good about yourself, about your life, about everything! Just like the definition for addiction says, you have surrendered yourself to a behavior that's habitual, obsessive, and impairs your vital functioning.[3]

But while some spend out of the compulsion of their emotional illness, most are merely victims who have fallen prey to the lure of advertising agencies. Clever marketing is what has trapped them. Such marketing has been compared to a ladder with a set number of steps. The challenge for advertisers is to get on one of the steps. The steps are limited, so the competition is fierce. Marketers deal in images and intend to make us slaves to those images. They deliberately and successfully manipulate our thinking without our even being aware. In the process, they blur the lines between needs and wants.

The speed at which we can be convinced to spend on such questionable necessities is amazing. Usually, it occurs instantaneously, for we live in an instant age. We have instant breakfast, instant cocoa, instant potatoes, instant indigestion, and instant relief. We have instant polling to tell us what we believe. We have instant loans, instant credit, instant cash, and instant success. We have hotlines and Web sites to solve all of our problems. We can receive instant weather forecasts, movie schedules, and educational advice. Students can receive instant online help with their homework and no longer require the assistance of Mom and Dad. By writing or e-mailing for free materials, we can receive near-instantaneous formulas for success in a variety of fields. And with just one silver dollar, you could become instantly rich in the state of Nevada.

Even in building intimate and lasting relationships, there is the instant approach. Perfume and aftershave make us instantly attractive, shampoos offer instant romance, and designer jeans instantly hold the opposite sex captive. Happiness is yours, say the advertisers, and it is priceless!

In a sense, we might say that we have all been seduced by the swipe of a credit card and have forgotten that sage advice offered by Frederick Keonig: "Happiness doesn't come as a result of getting something we don't have, but rather of recognizing and appreciating what we do have."[4]

Chapter 15

# Adjusting Your Income and Expenses in Turbulent Times

"We are built," observed Maxwell Maltz, author of *Psycho-Cybernetics,* "to conquer environment, solve problems, achieve goals, and we find no real satisfaction or happiness in life without obstacles to conquer and goals to achieve."[1]

Life has been good to us the past few decades. Incomes rose and jobs were plentiful. We could easily change employment and find ever-increasing opportunity. If we didn't have money, we at least had credit cards. Financing was affordable and credit flowed. We had growing 401(k)s and the world was at our feet.

Until recently, it never occurred to many of us that an economy is as fragile as pie crust can be. We should have asked some crucial questions along our easy path, but they never occurred to us. Am I prepared for this moment? Suppose I lose my job? What if a family member were to face catastrophic illness? Could I afford adequate health care? What if the entire economy turns on its head? Do we have enough to get through the hard times? How much should I be saving to protect against the storms of life?

If this day finds you facing some tough decisions—if your financial health is in need of help—the first part of this chapter is for you. We will assess your financial health in three stages and offer suggestions for coping with each stage.

# Financial Health

Financial health is like our physical well-being. When we are young, we think we'll live forever. When we are young and inexperienced, we make this same assumption when it comes to financial well-being. We think that our finances and our economy will only improve year by year.

Do you remember those happy, carefree days before you realized that in time you would certainly face health crises in your life? Perhaps this realization came when you were involved in your first automobile accident. Perhaps that accident wasn't too serious and you left the emergency room with only a few cuts, a stitch or two, and a lot more wisdom and caution than when you entered.

Perhaps the next encounter with mortality came with a sudden life-threatening illness. I (Lyle) faced one of those. I remember how, the previous day, I had been reflecting on how wonderful life was and how content I was with my robust health, and then—BAM! Like a bolt from the blue, I felt a sudden and crushing pain in my chest. I denied the obvious at first, attributing my problems to a bad case of indigestion. But before long I realized that I was having a heart attack. Fortunately, a great team of doctors worked tirelessly to pull me through. Eventually I returned to full health a whole lot wiser, more cautious, and much more attentive to the rules of good health.

Sometimes we are not so lucky as to have only a minor auto accident or just a brush with death; sometimes we stare death in the face. We have all had a friend, a neighbor, a coworker, or a family member who was the picture of health one day but battling for life the next day. As we watched our friend or loved one suffer, we suffered as well. Sometimes the person pulled through; other times the person lost the battle.

We experience similar situations in our economic life. Sometimes we get careless and find ourselves involved in a not-too-serious financial accident. Maybe we were blindsided or made a mistake we could have prevented. Maybe we were not even at fault. Ultimately, it didn't matter. It was not too serious; we learned from it and moved on.

Sometimes we suffer from a more serious situation that is not life-threatening in an economic way—something akin to my heart attack. We notice the symptoms soon enough to remedy the situation. We make adjustments, some of which are painful, and move on.

Sometimes, however, our situation borders on terminal. We have to do everything within our power just to survive. The measures we take are painful, and the climb out is long and hard. The cure might even, for a time, affect our family's well-being. But in financial peril, even in the most terminal of circumstances, there is a resurrection clause. After our term of suffering ends, we can pick ourselves up and start over. That is, we can do so if we manage to keep our faith and hope alive.

# Steps to Financial Health

When we find ourselves engulfed in serious financial circumstances, we tend to beat ourselves up. We think that somehow we are less as human beings. We think we are no longer good people. We mourn and lose all self-respect. If this describes your situation and behavior, take heart. Financial difficulties can come to good people who have the best of intentions. Even if we feel we are totally to blame, we have to stop beating on ourselves. Such actions are counterproductive. Instead, we must roll up our sleeves and get to work. No matter how mild or how serious our situation, there are steps we can take to return to full financial health. Our survival depends on our faith, our determination, and our hard work. It also depends on our continued faith in God. Look over the following scenarios for suggestions that will prove beneficial to your situation.

## Diagnose Your Financial Condition

Just as when you're battling an illness, the first step you take to achieving financial health is to diagnose your current circumstances. Just how bad is your trouble?

Begin by gathering your paperwork (we'll tell you what you need). Then sit down alone if you are single or with your spouse if you are married and look at the big picture. We cannot stress enough that *if you are married, you absolutely cannot assess the situation without including your spouse!* This is going to be a painful process, but it must be done.

*Start with your resources.* What is your salary? Can you expect a bonus this year? What about income tax refunds, birthday cash gifts, Christmas presents? Do you have any savings accounts from which you can draw? Do you have any assets you can sell? Write down your income and your prospective income. Be pessimistic rather than optimistic. It is better to prepare for the worst and hope for the best.

*List your liabilities.* Begin by recording your essential living expenses: mortgage, food, utilities, taxes, and anything else that is indispensable. You have to pay these bills first.

Then move from living expenses to debts. If you have no debt, your chances of financial survival, whatever your situation, are very good. However, this is generally not the case. Most people do carry some amount of debt. Recording your debts will undoubtedly be a painful process. Record every bill—and we do mean *every* one.

Some couples may have secret credit cards and secret balances. We'll discuss this in the next chapter. If you have accounts your spouse knows nothing about or balances your spouse has not seen, this is the moment to come clean. *Resist the temptation to blame.*

Find a notebook or a financial program, or use the computer program and spreadsheets we provided in our first book. Write down your debts and your creditors, the interest rates, and the minimum payments. If you have our first book, *Debt-Free on Any Income*, you will find debt-recording worksheets onto which you can record your debts. Your survival depends on obtaining a clear picture of your situation. It's just as important that you maintain hope in the process. So remember, clarity is the first step; hope is the second. You have to know, and you have to believe.

*Get your credit report.* Viewing your situation is only the first part of obtaining a diagnosis. You also need to see how others view your financial situation. You can do this by obtaining a credit report. You can get free reports once a year by going to www.AnnualCreditReport.com provided by the Federal Trade Commission (www.ftc.gov/). The credit report provides you with very valuable information. Check out the Web site section titled "Frequently Asked Questions" for some real helps on understanding your credit report and why it is important. Some companies advertise that they can obtain a free credit report for you, but always consult their fine print. Many that advertise free credit reports actually bill you every month once you have signed up for their service. Do not pay for a free credit report!

Three consumer credit-reporting companies provide free reports: Equifax (www.equifax.com), Experian (www.experian.com), and TransUnion (www.transunion.com). For about $6 you can get a credit score by which you will be judged when you apply for a credit card or a loan from a bank or when you try to buy a new car. Your credit score is worth knowing because it reveals the way other financial institutions look at you. It does not necessarily reveal everything as you might still be up to your neck in debt and have a high score because you have managed to keep current on your obligations. But these reports do give you a part of the total picture and are, as such, important for you to review because they will affect the interest rate you are charged by a creditor.

Once you have a score, you also need to know how to interpret it. If your credit score is 760 points or above, you are considered to have an "A" on your credit report. This entitles you to the best credit rates. Anything below that but still above 700 is considered to be a "B." If your score is between 600 and 700, you get a "C." Below 600 you have a "D," and lower than that would be considered a failing grade. The lower the credit rating, the higher the interest rates. To lower the interest rates of your credit cards, you need to lower your score by paying off balances and whittling down your debt.

Credit reports can contain errors. Look over your report carefully, and if you spot an error, report it immediately. Credit reports are also good for spotting identity theft. We will discuss this later on in this chapter.

In addition to consulting your credit report, you may want to consult another Web site: www.bankrate.com. This site contains lots of helps for your finances. You'll find calculators and financial assistance on everything from budgeting to debt management. Take a peek at it, and keep the resources there in mind as you move through the remaining steps to recovery.

## Choose Your Level of Cure

The level of your treatment depends upon the seriousness of your sickness. Whatever the circumstance and whatever the level of cure, there must be great effort. Henry David Thoreau counseled, "You must not only aim right, but draw the bow with all your might."[2] We'll illustrate.

*The aspirin cure.* If you can manage your own finances without help but you experience occasional sleepless nights worrying over your financial state, you probably require no more than an aspirin.

*Learn to budget.* If you've never budgeted before, begin with a spending plan. You'll find detailed information on how to budget wisely in chapter 8 of *Debt-Free on Any Income.* In review, a successful budget requires that you start a year in advance so that you can balance peak incomes with peak expenses, realizing that no month's expenses are the same. In addition, expense categories ought to be detailed enough so that you do not neglect to include all of your necessary expenses. The little surprises can destroy your best-laid plan. If you are budgeting successfully, you can minimize unexpected expenses by keeping a record of any surprises you encounter each month. By the time it comes to planning next year's budget, things will go more smoothly with a record of such expenses. Also, remember that maintaining too rigid a budget will only frustrate you. Always keep a little surplus in your budget.

*Track your spending.* In addition to planning your spending, record it. Keeping track of each week's expenses will take only a few minutes out of your busy schedule, and each minute you spend will pay big dividends. The only way to successfully budget is to track your expenditures and assess your current status each week. Be sure to include your spouse.

*Adjust your spending habits.* Aspirin therapy also requires that you adjust your spending habits when needed, keep tighter restraints on impulse spending, save a little money against emergencies, and develop good financial habits in general.

*The therapy cure.* This state is a little more serious. You are experiencing some real pain, and you may even feel that you are bleeding out of control. You have so many expenses that a budget can't handle them. This is where you need to make some tough decisions.

*Find additional income.* You may need to find a second job in order to generate additional resources. Perhaps both you and your spouse, if you're not doing so already, may have to work at least temporarily. This is a last option, however, if the wife's job requires that children be left alone during critical times. Carefully heed the advice of your priesthood leaders.

*Sell some of your assets.* You can trade in your expensive car for a less-expensive one; you might even consider parking the car and taking public transportation. You also might consider foregoing the purchase of things you had planned on—new carpet, new furniture, new appliances—and making do with what you have. Do you have any valuables that can be turned into cash? Can you sell used clothing at a consignment store or post it on eBay? What about photographic equipment, camping equipment, musical instruments? This will undoubtedly be painful, but it may be necessary. The therapy cure requires sincere commitment, effort, and sacrifice.

*Consult with professionals.* With a therapy cure, you may need a financial physician—the proper specialist to fit your individual needs. There are tax accountants, investment counselors, lawyers, and personal money-management specialists. In addition, there are classes you can take through extension or continuing-education services. Don't neglect to speak with advisers who may be provided through your bank or credit union. Speak with bishops, stake presidents, and knowledgeable friends. Get all the information you can. Knowledge is power. Even if professional advice costs a dollar or two, it will be worth it.

*Major-surgery cure.* This is the cure for those who are fighting for their financial life. If you need this cure, you are probably hemorrhaging and require critical care and professional help to rescue you. You might have to relocate, seek a better job, or downsize your house. You may have to go to a debt-counseling service to assist you in negotiating your debt with your creditors. You may have to implement severe budget restrictions.

*Plead your case.* If you can't pay your bills, first go to your financial institutions and creditors and plead your case. You may have to go up the ladder, starting with those who will give you no hope for relief. Ask for their supervisor, then ask for the customer relations office, then ask for the hardship department. Indicate that you are having a difficult time paying your bill. This could raise a red flag with your credit card company, but if you are in desperate need and are willing to do what you can to solve this problem, this is an important first step. Ask for lower payments, more time to pay, a lower interest rate, and the removal of penalties. Each charge you can remove from your bill may prove critical. Write yourself a script, or jot down talking points. Be kind and polite, but remain firm and resolved. Don't react even if the person becomes abusive. Some employees are trained to turn you off. Don't be dissuaded with the first rejection; keep trying. Work down your list of creditors, and don't get discouraged because a couple of them turn you down. Keep asking.

*Find certified professional credit counselors.* If you receive no help by dealing with your creditors yourself, take the next step. Find a certified professional to negotiate for you. Debt-management services can be found in the phone book or on the Internet. State divisions of consumer protection keep a list of certified professionals in your area. You can obtain the list with a call or by checking online. State divisions are not available in all states, but you can find similar agencies through credit-counseling services.

Watch out for quacks; they could leave you in worse condition than when you began. Above all, check the rating of companies with the Better Business Bureau at www.bbb.org. Counseling services should be rated with letter grades, from A + to F, with an explanation for the reason for their rating. Deal only with companies that have earned an A rating.

Here is a list of qualifications for responsible credit counselors:

- They are properly licensed and bonded.
- They spend at least thirty minutes talking to you about your finances before they suggest a debt-management plan.
- They have a solid record with the Better Business Bureau.
- They have been in business long enough to have a good reputation.
- They provide prompt monthly statements.
- They offer educational resources to help you stay out of debt.
- They employ experienced certified counselors.
- They provide account access twenty-four hours a day.
- They have an electronic payment process linked to creditors.
- They already have relationships with most creditors.
- They offer multiple options to help you get out of debt.

- They have a support network that connects with other community partners.
- They offer a reasonable fee structure based on ability to pay.[3]

*Write a debt-payment plan.* With the help of your certified professional, you should develop a debt-management plan. Some credit counselors will charge you a fee, but their fee should be less than what you might pay in penalties and overdue fines. Avoid any counseling service that charges excessive fees.

*Bankruptcy.* Unfortunately, we cannot leave out the worst-case scenario, major surgery cure. We speak of bankruptcy. When every resource has been exhausted and all else fails, you may have to declare bankruptcy. Bankruptcy is a last-ditch resort, but as stated earlier, it comes with a resurrection clause after you suffer some initial pain. Make no mistake; this is a painful solution that must be considered only after everything else has failed. Bankruptcy has long-term results. Here are a few of them:

- Bankruptcy will be on your credit report for up to ten years.
- Many of your personal belongings will be sold or turned back to creditors.
- It will be difficult if not impossible to get credit to buy a home or a car.
- It could affect your ability to get a job.
- It costs money to file bankruptcy, pay lawyers, cover court costs, pay filing fees, and so forth.

If you are considering this step, you should consult with a good bankruptcy attorney, who will be aware of the related laws that have changed in the past few years. Here is a short and incomplete summary of what you can expect:

In October 2005, Congress made sweeping changes to bankruptcy laws. The net effect of these changes is to give consumers more incentive to seek bankruptcy relief under Chapter 13 rather than under Chapter 7. Chapter 13 allows people with a steady income to keep property like a mortgaged house or car that they might otherwise lose through Chapter 7. In Chapter 13, the court approves a repayment plan that allows you to use your future income to pay off your debts during a three-to-five-year period rather than to surrender any property. After you have made all the payments under the plan, you receive a discharge of your debts.

Chapter 7 is known as straight bankruptcy and involves liquidation of all assets that are not exempt. Exempt property may include automobiles, work-related tools, and basic household furnishings. Some of your property may be sold by a court-appointed official—a trustee—or turned over to your creditors. The new bankruptcy laws have changed the time period during which you can receive a discharge of debt through Chapter 7. You must now wait eight years after receiving a discharge through Chapter 7 before you can file again under that chapter. The Chapter 13 waiting period is much shorter and can be as little as two years between filings.

Both types of bankruptcy may rid you of unsecured debts and stop foreclosures, repossessions, garnishments, debt-collection activities, and the shutting off of utilities. Both also provide exemptions that allow people to keep certain assets, although exemption amounts vary by state. Note that personal bankruptcy usually does not erase child support, alimony, fines, taxes, and some student loan obligations. And unless you have an acceptable plan to catch up on your debt under Chapter 13, bankruptcy usually does not allow you to keep property when your creditor has an unpaid mortgage or security lien on it.[4]

*Get your credit cards under control.* We cannot conclude this chapter on coping with tough times without a general discussion about gaining control of your credit cards. Credit cards can be amazing tools if used properly, or they can be like poison to your financial health. To be financially secure, you must gain control of your credit cards. Pending legislation may alter existing regulations, but as a good rule of thumb, adhere to the following advice.

*Select the right card for your circumstances or level of willpower.* Not all cards are the same. Some require that you pay them in full at the end of every month, some allow you to carry a balance with interest over an extended period of time, and some are designed to deduct funds directly from your bank account. To ensure your safety and to hedge against a decline in willpower, you should avoid any card that carries a balance that accrues interest.

Use exclusively those cards that are to be paid in full at the end of every month such as debit or bank cards that are deducted directly from your checking account. If for business purposes you are required to keep a card with a credit balance, make it a practice to pay it in full far in advance of your payment's due date to avoid interest and late fees.

*Consolidate bills to pay off credit card balances.* If you have a credit card debt with high interest and haven't paid off the balance, you might consider some sort of bill consolidation at a lower interest rate while you pay off the debt. But stay away from any finance company that offers quick fixes and high interest rates. If your debt consolidation involves using your home as collateral, be wary. You can jeopardize your family's future by risking your home unnecessarily.

*Employ the roll-down method.* The surest way to eliminate debt is by the roll-down method we call the *power payment plan* outlined in our book *Debt-Free on Any Income.* Whether your financial sickness is mild or severe, begin to get your credit cards under control by putting them away. Do not use them again—not until they are under control and perhaps never again if you feel you cannot trust yourself with them.

*Examine your statement and dispute erroneous charges.* Keep credit receipts in an accessible place just as you do your bills. Carefully and thoroughly review your credit card statements each month, and verify each purchase. Look for hidden costs you didn't anticipate. Dispute any erroneous charges. Be aware of every charge, and report anything that looks like identity theft or credit card fraud.

*Watch out for identity theft.* Identity theft is becoming a major problem in this country as unscrupulous people steal private information and pass themselves off as someone else. "Identity theft is one of the fastest-growing crimes in the United States, with about 75,000 cases per year (according to an estimate from the Privacy Rights Clearinghouse). Typically, the perpetrator steals the Social Security number of the victim and enough other information to apply for credit cards, mobile phone accounts, or other services. The bills are diverted to a new address, and the charges pile up. According to the Federal Trade Commission, the average debt amounts to $17,000. While victims are protected by law from having to pay fraudulent charges, their credit ratings suffer enormous damage that may take years to repair."[5]

Never give out your credit card numbers to unknown vendors, and protect yourself by destroying any documents or carbon sales slips that list your credit card number. Don't give out your credit card number to a solicitor you didn't seek out first, and don't do business with vendors you are not familiar with.

Those who have become victims know that identity theft is a long and painful ride. Unsuspecting victims have found themselves in jail, the subject of lawsuits, and in debt for things they never purchased. Of course, you do not ultimately have to pay these fraudulent charges, but while you battle to resolve the problem, your life can be a living nightmare. You can protect yourself from identity theft by doing the following:

- Look at your credit report regularly and see that no mystery transactions have taken place.

- Invest in a cheap shredder and use it.

- Fill out a change-of-address card if you move. If you leave town, always have someone pick up your mail or have the post office hold it for you.

- Report lost credit cards immediately. Know the contents of your wallet or purse in case it is stolen.

- Be careful what you share over the Internet—never order anything without security protection. Use an e-card.

- Be careful what you share over the telephone.

- Don't use a debit card online.

- Know when your monthly statements arrive, and if they don't come—even if you have a zero balance—check to make sure someone didn't steal them and change your address.

- Notify the police immediately if you think your identity has been stolen.

- Don't use identifying information that thieves can easily obtain such as a maiden name, a birth date, or a place of birth.

- Warn your kids about privacy on the Internet.

- If a Web site says it won't operate without a cookie, don't believe it.

- Mail payments at the post office and not from unsecured mailboxes.[6]

*Cut fees and charges.* In addition to looking for erroneous charges and identity theft, examine your statement for any services that your credit card company might automatically charge—particularly those you no longer require or those you were only trying out temporarily. Examples of these kinds of charges are magazine subscriptions offered on a trial basis or special programs offered on an introductory basis. If these programs and subscriptions are not beneficial to you, ask that they be canceled. Most companies will comply with your request just by a simple phone call.

*Pay your credit card bills on time.* If you pay late, expect higher interest rates, penalties, and fees "without notice." That is because under old regulations, credit card companies were allowed to change interest rates without notice and to assess fees and penalties, even hidden penalties, without having to disclose them to you in advance. The "without notice" rule will still be in effect until February 2010, but after that date new regulations will take effect. From that point on, cardholders will be given a notice of forty-five days of any rate increase on their account. There will be no more hair-trigger losses of promotional rates, no hiking of rates on cards that are less than thirty days late, and no forcing you to pay in full the lowest-interest portion of your balance before the higher-interest portion can be paid. This describes the situation many cardholders have found themselves in when they transferred balances to a new card. Often a competing card company offered 0.0 % interest on balance transfers, but if the cardholder had to take out an emergency loan for an additional amount, that amount was charged at a higher rate. Until the balance transfer was paid in full, the higher interest on the new charges kept accruing.

In addition, new regulations allow you twenty-one days from the time a card is mailed to you until your payment is due, and you will no longer be assessed a two-cycle billing in which a finance charge is calculated based in part on balances you have already paid. There will also be no interest rate increases during the first year after an account is opened unless the cardholder is informed at that time what the new rate will be and when it will start. Other new regulations will be discussed as we proceed.

Credit card companies are required to send you, at least annually, a disclosure statement on their rules and regulations. These statements are generally written in small print and in language so complex that it requires a truckload of lawyers to interpret it. Because they are designed to look like advertisements so as to be overlooked by the consumer, never throw things away without first carefully looking at them. To show you the wealth of information you can glean from these statements, consider this one in fine print: "We may obtain information such as your Internet service provider, your e-mail address, your computer's operating system and Web browser, your Web site use and your product and service preferences from your visits to Web sites."

Here's another quotation to make you nervous: "Sharing Personal Information with Our Corporate Family. . . . We may share the information we collect about you as described in Section One with other members of our corporate family."[7] Who is the company's corporate family? Part of the family is other credit card companies and consumer credit-reporting companies that provide your credit information to anyone that inquires. One other thing: If you are late on a payment, not only will the company hike your interest rate, but its corporate family with whom the company shares your information may as well. This is an area where we need some legislation to protect our privacy.

*Look for changing due dates.* Have you ever wondered why your credit card statements have due dates in the middle of the month? It is because most bills come due at either the beginning or the end of the month. Being creatures of habit, we may not think to look over our credit card statements in the middle of the month. This allows card companies to make a little extra money through late fees. In the past a late payment on even one card could cause *universal default,* a term that means that if even one credit card is late and is reclassified as high-risk, all other cards held by the same cardholder could also legally be reclassified a high-risk. High-risk means higher interest rates—as high as 30 percent. When such rates extend to all cards, customers can go from financially secure to financially unable to meet minimum payments in just a matter of months.

Beware that online services can and often do go down just before a payment's due date. Computers are unreliable. When a server is down and it's too late to mail a payment, you have no other option but to pay over the phone. Phone fees for credit cards can be as much as half the late-payment fee.

With new regulations come new and perhaps unanticipated

results. Many experts predict that credit card companies will make up for revenue lost by the new regulations by raising late-payment fees to $150. Therefore, it will be absolutely essential that you watch your statements, and, if possible, even monitor your balances online to ensure that they are paid before deadlines.

*Do not exceed credit limits.* Be careful to never exceed your credit limit. If you exceed it even once, additional fees will be charged to your account. Such fees have been known to cause original debt to double or even triple. In the past, credit limits could be reduced without warning. But by February 2010, a new law will give cardholders a notice of forty-five days on any new credit limits. In addition, once the new law takes effect, over-limit fees caused by a card company's hold on available credit will not be assessed, and there will also be limits to the number of over-limit fees that can be charged a single account in a month.

*Lower your credit card interest.* Keep debts under control and choose your cards wisely. Most experts advise that your interest rate should never exceed 9.9 percent. Search the Internet to find a list of cards with low rates. Remain wary. Make sure the low rates are not just an initial lure that jumps abruptly after a trial period. Low-rate cards can jump much higher than the rates you may be accustomed to paying. Read all the fine print. Ask that your minimum payments be as high as you can afford, or just make it a point of always paying more than the minimum payment.

*Consider using cash instead.* This is particularly true when you know you need a surer form of discipline. When you are out of money, you are out of money.

It really feels good to sleep at night. There is a peace that comes once we put our financial house in order. With that peace comes freedom. The burden lifts and we can breathe again. President Gordon B. Hinckley said it best:

> What a wonderful feeling it is to be free of debt. . . .
> I urge you, brethren, to look to the condition of your
> finances. I urge you to be modest in your expenditures;

discipline yourselves in your purchases to avoid debt to the extent possible. Pay off debt as quickly as you can, and free yourselves from bondage. . . . If you have paid your debts, if you have a reserve, even though it be small, then should storms howl about your head, you will have shelter for your wives and children and peace in your hearts. That's all I have to say about it, but I wish to say it with all the emphasis of which I am capable.[8]

# Chapter 16

# Financial
# Fidelity

Louis K. Anspacher observed, "Marriage is that relation between man and woman in which the independence is equal, the dependence mutual, and the obligation reciprocal."[1] That describes a perfect world.

In what many believe to be a perfect world, the husband has a job that he loves. He provides for his family in such a way that they never lack the things they need, and there is often money left over to supply wants. The family dwells in comfort. They have no problem meeting their bills. They have sufficient money that the husband and wife never need to check with one another before buying something. If she would like a new car, she goes out, picks the make and color she wants, and she buys it. The husband has the same prerogative. He may even come home one afternoon and announce, "Guess what? I just bought a new boat for the family."

The wife is excited. She responds, "That is wonderful, dear. I am so delighted and happy. Oh, by the way, did you see our new car in the driveway?" He responds, "That's great. I hope you'll consider it yours. You needed one!"

That seems to be the perfect world. But is that the way it goes in your house? Perhaps at your house it is the exact opposite. Money is always in short supply. Any purchase results in an argument:

"You bought toothpaste again? What are you trying to do, drive us to the poorhouse?"

"You aren't going golfing again? I can't even buy milk for the baby!"

This is not the way to have a full and happy life. We all know the statistics. Figures differ, but experts agree that the elephant in the room in most marriages is money matters, and no one wants to talk about it until it spirals out of control. So the financial elephant stays in the room and grows bigger than life day by day, and yet the husband and wife still refuse to talk about it.

This chapter deals with a serious problem—a growing situation experts call *financial infidelity.* It works this way: She goes shopping at the store and sees a toy she would like to buy for the kids. She knows it is not in the budget. She thinks it over, saying to herself, "He will never know, and it is only a couple of bucks." So she buys it and takes it home. The husband comes home and sees his son playing with it and he asks, "Where did you get that?" Just then the wife walks in. "Oh, Grandpa bought it for him." She lies. She knows the truth will start a fight.

He is just as bad. He buys a Blackberry and he lies, saying, "I need this for my business." His laptop does everything his Blackberry does, and there is no monthly fee associated with the laptop. He even realizes that the service fee may put the family budget in jeopardy, but he doesn't care. He loves his new toy, and he doesn't want to give it up.

Don't get us wrong. We are not opposed to electronic toys that make our lives more pleasant. But we *are* opposed to fighting and lying to a spouse, a parent, or even yourself about the way you spend money.

# What Do We Fight About?

According to a 2005 Harris Interactive Survey, 50 percent of families surveyed said spending money on themselves was one of the money issues they face. Other money issues included the following:

- Managing the household budget: 45 percent
- Paying off credit card debt: 32 percent
- Spending money on the kids: 26 percent
- Planning for retirement: 10 percent
- Determining how to invest: 7 percent
- Spending on kids' education: 5 percent
- Other financial issues: 21 percent

Fighting can lead to lying, and lying can lead to financial infidelity. Psychologist Karen Sherman addresses the problem.

The biggest financial problem that couples have, one would think, is the typical how are we going to spend our money on the big items or balancing the checkbook, but it's really financial infidelity.

Question: Why is financial infidelity such a marriage killer?

Well, because it's such a total breach of trust in the marriage; it's a total breakdown of the relationship and the trust that has been the fountain of the marriage.

Question: Why is it more devastating than, say, a sexual affair?

Well you know, obviously when one has a typical affair then that is humiliating, it's horrible, but in many cases it's an indicator that there's something wrong in the marriage, and it can be used as a springboard for finding out what was wrong in the marriage. When there is financial infidelity it's one person who has done it, and it's something about that person, and it's not indicative about something that is really wrong in the marriage and so it's really very hard to repair.[2]

*Financial fidelity* can be defined as faithfulness to obligations, duties, and observances or honesty in money matters with those who have claim on our resources.

A 2005 survey conducted by lawyers.com and *Redbook* magazine, commissioned by Harris Interactive, tells the tale. After interviews with 1,796 married, engaged, or couples ages twenty-five to fifty-five who were living together, here is what the survey found:

- Virtually all the people interviewed (96 percent) said it was both partners' responsibility to be completely honest about financial issues.

- Nearly one in four (24 percent) believed so strongly in the principle of financial fidelity that they said openness about money is *more* important than being sexually faithful. (As lawyers.com legal editor Alan Kopit put it, "They're saying, 'It's one thing to fool around. It's another thing to fool around with my hard-earned cash!'")

- Almost one in three (29 percent) admitted that they had lied to their partner about finances, most often about personal spending (21 percent) or spending on the kids (12 percent).

- One in four (25 percent) said a partner has withheld financial information, usually about personal spending (20 percent) and spending on children (11 percent).

# Why Do We Lie?

The reason most people stretch the truth is to save face. Self-protection is a pride issue, and we all know what pride leads to. We sometimes wrongly assume that if we ignore our money woes, they will magically disappear. Such assumptions always backfire. The problem continues to fester and eventually becomes an eruption. Then the truth comes out, trust is destroyed, and questions plague the relationship, including, "What else is my partner not telling me?"

Most of the lies we tell begin with ourselves when we repeat the things we've whispered in our hearts to our spouses. Sometimes our lies are silence; we simply fail to report what we know we must. Rationalized omission is only another kind of lie.

Let's look at a sampling of the sorts of things couples rationalize and lie about:

- "It's only a small amount, and the minimum payment isn't much."

- "I bring in most of the income, so I deserve a little more to spend."

- "Everyone has one of these."

- "If Joe can afford it, so can I."

- "My kids need one of these."

- "Spending a little once in a while makes me feel better."

- "I'll only do it this once."

- "No one will ever know."

- "It's nobody's business how I spend my money."

- "The payment is in the mail."

- "We have just had a hard month, and I am getting a raise."

- "We deserve to have this and live better."

- "He (or she) doesn't love me because they won't let me buy . . ."

- "This is on sale, and if I don't buy it now I will lose money."

- "I do not need to seek professional advice; I can work it out myself."

We know these excuses are not true the minute we offer them, but we dare not tell the truth even to ourselves. Clever advertisers assuage our guilt. Friends on a shopping spree tease us into spending. So we spend and spend. We lie about the purchase, and we hide the credit card statements when they arrive. We pay whatever we can, we continue to spend, and the lies grow deeper. But then one day reality smacks us in the face. We extend our card to pay for stuff we don't really want and can't really afford, and the clerk delivers the awful news: "Your credit has been declined." We cower in shame. We do not want anyone to know what we have done. The last thing we want to do is tell the person we love the most, "Yep, I've been financially unfaithful."

# Financial Fidelity

Financial fidelity is just the opposite. We can be loyal and true, even in matters of money. It is never too early to start, and it is never too late to change.

Couples need to discuss financial matters even before they get married. They need to sit together and form goals. They need to talk about dreams. They need to look at present realities. Engaged couples need to discuss with each other any financial entanglements. Debts and liabilities must be transparent. Educational loans, automobile loans, and credit card balances all have to be discussed prior to the marriage. Savings accounts should be open to review. There must be discussions about needs and wants. Couples should enter marriage with their eyes wide open.

Once a couple begins their life together, all their assets should be shared. From the first week, finances should be a joint partnership. Budgets should be established under a mutual agreement. Checking accounts, savings accounts, and retirement accounts should be joint, not separate. If couples begin their marriage this way, they will establish a pattern that will allow them to work out small problems so that when the big ones come, and they will, they will know they can handle them—together.

Perhaps you have been married for years. Perhaps you have kept a few secrets. It is not too late to make necessary changes. Today is the day when secrets must come to an end. Today is the day to talk about the elephant in the room. There can be no blaming, no tantrums, and no hysterics. Solutions are found as a team, not solo. Man and wife must sing a duet.

# Budget Is Still the Key

In nearly every chapter, we have explained the importance of planning your spending together. This is doubly true when it comes to achieving and maintaining financial fidelity. Set an established time each week to work together on your finances. Make it a pleasant and uninterrupted atmosphere.

I once counseled a young couple who refused to communicate about their money. One of them told me, "We can't work on a budget. It creates way too much contention, and contention hurts." It was a lie, and I knew it. The contention came because they never did talk about it. They felt secure keeping their secrets. Each was afraid the other would find out about the spending and the credit cards each had kept secret. They knew that if they talked, their secret spending would have to end, and they were insecure about the exposure of their secrets.

It was true that the initial disclosure might have caused a few feelings, but in time, with love and a lack of blame, they could have worked through things. I could see a deep and growing anger inside these individuals. Their silence was like a volcano just before eruption. They could not foresee that eventually all their secrets would be revealed and that those secrets would hurt far less if the exposure of them came not from someone outside the relationship but from the loved ones within it.

President N. Eldon Tanner delivered some sound advice that, if heeded, leads to financial fidelity. He urged couples to "pay an honest tithing, live on less than you earn, learn to distinguish between needs and wants, develop and live within a budget, and be honest in all your financial dealings." These five principles, he explained, will bless us and "bring financial security and peace of mind under *any* economic circumstances."[3]

It may seem strange, but if the family budgeting session begins with a prayer, the chances are smaller that there will be contention. It is hard to have disputes about money matters when the Holy Ghost is present. Explain to the Lord any problems with which you might be grappling. To God there are no temporal matters. Can there be any greater financial adviser than the Creator of the universe? With God all things are possible.

Use this time to exchange not just dollars and cents but also feelings. Establish priorities, talk about goals, and plan your strategies. Balance your checkbook, pay your bills, work on your budget, and give yourself a financial report. This is not a time to proceed on either impulse or emotion.

Problems are easy to solve when we listen and employ common sense. What can be more valuable than that look of love in the eyes of the one you love? Three words solve nearly every economic crisis: communicate, communicate, communicate.

Financial infidelity destroys relationships; financial fidelity builds them.

# Chapter 17

# Coping with Unemployment and Underemployment

The future is uncertain. What lies ahead for us and for our families? No one knows for sure. At some time or another in our life we will undoubtedly find ourselves either unemployed or underemployed—perhaps both. Such situations are always agonizing and often confidence-shattering, but we will eventually find new employment and will emerge in better shape than we were before. In the meantime we can hedge against such days by becoming valuable employees.

My father taught me the value of being a good employee. Perhaps your father taught you the same. My father never had the privilege of gaining more than a sixth-grade education, yet he was one of the wisest men I have ever known. Two lessons I learned from him have guided my life. First, learn to work with both your head *and* your hands. If anything ever happens to your head, you will be able to work with your hands. If anything ever happens to your hands, you will be able to work with your head. Second, you are not as smart as the next guy, so you will just have to outwork him.

*Learn to work with your head as well as your hands.* What my father said in his own simple way was something rather remarkable. It was no less profound than the words of the great psychologist William James, who said: "The greatest discovery of my generation is that you can change your circumstances by changing your mind."[1]

The most widespread disease in the world is the disease of inferiority. We may not all have the mental acumen of a rocket scientist, but the world needs more than rocket scientists. It needs businessmen, carpenters, doctors, plumbers, and so forth. Each of us has our niche, and each niche is essential. Imagination along with hard work is what separates success from failure.

Abraham Lincoln was defeated time and again in his pursuit of public office. Encouraged by a friend to make a run for the presidency, he succeeded. He saved the Union from ruin during the dark days of the Civil War, and he became one of the greatest presidents in U.S. history. When Walt Disney applied at a Kansas City newspaper for a job as an artist, the editor told him he didn't have any talent. When movie producers told Fred Astaire he had little talent for dancing, he refused to stop. When Albert Einstein was told by his teachers that he was stupid, he refused to believe it. You need to be able to use your head *and* your hands.

*Believe in yourself.* Keep telling yourself, "I am as good as anyone out there." Put a note on a mirror, and read it to yourself ten times a day if necessary. Don't worry about the past; create a future where positive things will happen. Steve Jobs, CEO of Apple Computers and former CEO of Pixar Animation Studios, once said of himself, "You can't connect the dots looking forward; you can only connect them looking backwards. So you have to trust that the dots will somehow connect in your future. You have to trust in something—your gut, destiny, life, karma, whatever. This approach has never let me down, and it has made all the difference in my life."[2]

Losing a job or being turned down for a promotion is something everyone has experienced more than once in life. Rejection, however, is not an excuse for losing focus and becoming discouraged. It should only add fuel to the fire. At such times a spouse can really lift a companion by constantly assuring the spouse that he or she is the smartest and best in the world. Nothing will wipe out a person's confidence faster than a spouse who beats the person to a pulp.

Being positive is the number one rule to being happy. I have hired many people, and I don't ever remember hiring a grump. In speaking of how he became successful, Steve Jobs said:

I'm pretty sure none of this [success] would have happened if I hadn't been fired from Apple. It was awful-tasting medicine, but I guess the patient needed it. Sometimes life hits you in the head with a brick. Don't lose faith. I'm convinced that the only thing that kept me going was that I loved what I did. You've got to find what you love. And this is as true for your work as it is for your lovers. Your work is going to fill a large part of your life, and the only way to be truly satisfied is to do what you believe is great work. And the only way to do great work is to love what you do. If you haven't found it yet, keep looking. Don't settle. As with all matters of the heart, you'll know when you find it. And, like any great relationship, it just gets better and better as the years roll on. So keep looking until you find it. Don't settle.[3]

*Analyze the job market.* You really need to analyze the job market and see where the jobs are. If you have a choice, pick something the world cannot do without. If one job market is down, another will be up. If the economy tanks, there is always one industry of another on the cutting edge of rising from the ashes. Find that job.

Scott was on the verge of buying his first business, a successful RV dealership, when the bottom dropped out of the market. He had spent six months working on the deal that would have been his first business. The opportunity had come, and it had gone, but he didn't give up or become discouraged. He started up his car one morning and went for a drive. He spotted an old service station that looked as if it had been abandoned for some time. He inquired about the owner and was directed to him.

What was it people needed with the downturn in the economy? RVs were not selling, and new cars were sitting on lots. He got an idea. People still needed to get to work, and old cars would still die and need replacing. How about selling something affordable? He went to work. He rented the old station and opened a used car lot that specialized in quality vehicles under $5,000. He became a success.

*Look for educational opportunities.* If you are searching for a career and have not settled on one, go to the local community college or university and get a catalog of courses. Pick the fields that interest you, and see what training is necessary to pursue the job of your dreams. Go after your dream as if your future financial life depended on it, because it probably does.

Take classes to further your education, and obtain the skills necessary for your dream vocation. Check for grants available for sharpening skills, or take advantage of educational incentives offered by your employer that could help you move into the job level or position you seek. Finding a new job is the same whether you are unemployed or underemployed.

*Update your job skills and further your education.* Each of us can update our job skills, keep current on trends in our profession, and prepare ourselves for the dreaded specter of unemployment. If you are in a job you love, you will want to do all within your power to keep your employer satisfied with your job performance. How do you do that? Well, take advantage of any educational seminars or opportunities to further your education, and consider earning a higher degree. Education eventually becomes income. It is the best investment you can possibly make. Whenever an employer offers you the possibility of furthering your job skills, take it. Whenever he offers an incentive for furthering your education, take it. Should you lose your job, you will have skills someone can use.

*Subscribe to professional or trade magazines.* Don't allow

yourself to become stagnant. Keep up with the latest trends and newest resources. Be selective in your subscriptions. Read only the most useful magazines. If your employer does not pay for these subscriptions or if you don't have the ability to pay, make the public library your friend. If the library does not carry the particular journals you want, your local college or university library may. Don't be afraid of a little hard work. Time spent sharpening your skills reaps big benefits.

*What if you don't like your job?* If you don't enjoy what you're doing, expend a little effort to find out where you will be happy. You might try *job shadowing,* which allows you to follow someone around who already works in the field that interests you. This will allow you to assess if the new profession is a better fit. Dreams can always become reality if you work for them. Never feel that you are trapped in a profession you abhor. Dare to dream big. Those who combine dreams with effort make dreams come true.

*Outwork the next guy.* When my dad gave me this bit of advice, I was disheartened. I thought at first he considered me a little dim-witted. I soon realized this was not the case. What I needed was a competitive edge, and he was giving it to me. I have learned over the years that hard work helps no matter how difficult times are. You have probably learned that too.

*Become the go-to person.* There is not only power in work, there is also joy. People who stay busy and engaged are the happiest people I know. A hard worker makes himself irreplaceable. By delivering more than what is asked, you make yourself secure. Do not be afraid of tough decisions either. Make certain you are always productive and efficient in whatever task you are assigned. It will not take long before you are recognized for your work ethic, and you will become the go-to person. Not only do you need to work hard, but you also need to work smart. Find out what your employer expects and deliver it. The scripture suggests that the laborer "is worthy of his hire" (D&C 31:5).

*Stay productive.* In the wonderful book *Fake Work,* authors Brent D. Peterson and Gaylan W. Nelson identify ways to be productive rather than spin your wheels and really not accomplish much. The first paragraph in the book describes wasted effort instead of real accomplishment:

> Suppose you are building a road on a mountainside leading to the site for your new cabin. You have worked for months clearing sagebrush and aspen trees. You've moved rocks and filled in roadbed through the exhausting heat, the raging downpours, even early snow. You've pushed forward, working from your best understanding of the surveyor's plans. Your road winds over a dusty hill, cuts through the trees, moves along a rock ridge, and then—you find yourself looking down from the edge of a cliff.
>
> Fake work looks and feels like that. The building of the road was purposeful. Your effort was admirable. The blood, sweat, and tears you poured into the project were real, and your commitment was profound. But none of that really matters. You are still left with a road to nowhere.[4]

*Don't be afraid to sweat.* My father had another favorite saying: "Don't trust a man who doesn't sweat." I learned that that referred to me as much as to the next guy. Work begets success.

# Preparing for Job Loss

In the army the drill sergeant would yell at us, "As you were!" That meant we should not move but stay fixed where we were. If times are uncertain, it is not the time to remodel the house or buy a recreational vehicle. Go back and reread chapter 3, "Do I Really Need This?" again. Dicey economic times require us to tighten our belt and hunker down. This means the whole family. Children may not be given all the perks they are used to. They may have to forgo a concert or a new iPod. Everyone needs to be included and asked to make small sacrifices, understanding that better days are ahead.

A good defense is always your best offense. If you've been paying attention to the suggestions in our earlier chapters, you'll know that you already have something to fall back on.

*Use your rainy-day fund.* The rainy day is here. If you've successfully saved three months of take-home pay, you can combine it with your unemployment compensation or your severance to get you by until you find another job.

*Prepare for the unexpected.* Be aware that severance packages are taxable income; don't let taxes blindside you. Consult with a good tax attorney to be sure you set aside enough of your severance to cover your taxes. Have him help you to manage and protect your resources during this down period. If your severance is sufficient to allow you to return to school, even part time to enhance your skills, take advantage of it. Educational expenses related to your line of work may be deductible and offset your tax liability. A little more education may help you launch a new career with higher wages. This is a time to be brave.

*Hang onto that raise.* Don't go right out and spend a raise if your job is uncertain. Bank it and live on what you have been earning. If you have a number of credit card debts, you might consider allocating some of the raise to those debts, particularly those with high-interest rates. Doing so would free up a few dollars each month and make life easier.

*Update your food supply.* Store things that will sustain life— just the basics such as grains, fats, sugar, salt, milk, and seeds. Buy a few hundred pounds of potatoes or perhaps a case of citrus. Peanut butter and tuna fish are also good items to store. Don't go into debt, but trim your food budget so you can buy and store some extra basics.

*Visit the doctor and dentist.* If you have health benefits that may be ending, schedule routine medical and dental checkups, and take care of your medical care needs while you are still covered.

*Maintain your health benefits.* Keep your medical insurance current so that health costs don't sink you. Losing insurance can be particularly harmful financially if a family member has a pre-existing condition. For that reason, experts recommend biting the bullet and taking the coverage offered by their former employer through COBRA. It's expensive because the individual pays what the coverage previously cost the individual and the former employer, plus 2 percent. But it provides the necessary continuity to maintain eligibility for medical insurance after the person finds a new job. Workers have sixty days to decide whether to accept COBRA coverage and can even wait until they have a claim to decide to take it. If a worker is young and healthy, he may want to look into getting an individual policy or coverage through a professional or trade association, counsels David Sommer, associate professor of risk management and insurance at the University of Georgia's Terry College of Business.[5]

*Contemplate your future.* Look at the end of a job as an opportunity to assess your present job satisfaction. Sit with your spouse and discuss frankly how you feel. Make a list of places you would like to work. Limit the list to five, and if you haven't already got contacts in these places, go find some. Don't tell your contacts that you are out of work or looking for a job; rather, ask for advice on the skills and character traits their business looks for. Everyone is happy to give advice, but many employers are guarded regarding employment opportunities. Advice is free.

*Consider a part-time job.* While you're looking for full-time work, you might find opportunities to do studies with research groups, apply for paid surveys, do pet sitting or babysitting, tutor for hire, work as a security guard, drive a school bus, type papers, deliver newspapers, stock shelves at the market, do home repairs, work as a clerk during the holiday season, or other such part-time jobs. Remember that if you spend too much time away from your family, you might develop serious family problems. It is better to cut back on your lifestyle than to sacrifice your family.

*Set up a family network.* Don't be proud. Inform your extended family that your employment may be coming to an end. Ask if there are things your family can do to assist you during these times. Your parents might be able to loan you some money. Sisters and sisters-in-law might volunteer to help with child care. Others might offer to help you with food storage. Family networks are valuable assets. Remember the Lord's law of economics and looking after one another.

*Cut unnecessary expenses.* We know we have covered this already, but repetition results in motivation. Look over your budget, and sort through each detail on your monthly bills. Look for any unnecessary expenses you can cut from your monthly budget. Limit or cut out the options on your phone bill. Cut your energy consumption. Find more efficient watering methods to trim the water bill, and so forth. There is fat in every family's budget that can be trimmed; when you're facing unemployment, it's time to trim to the bare bones. In addition, pay off all the debts you can as quickly as possible. Even if you owe no one but the mortgage company, you can survive on far less than you currently spend.

*Save vacation time.* If it looks as though you may lose your job, accrue as much vacation time as you can so you can have a little extra money to tide you over to the next job. Most employers cash out vacation time when they let people go. If the inevitable does happen, ask management for additional severance or golden parachutes even if they are not offered. If you have been a good employee, your employer may give you some extra help.

# Coping with Job Loss

Move on as quickly as possible. Don't beg or grovel. Keep your emotions in check. Don't burn any bridges; you might return some day, or perhaps someone within the company might recommend you. Thank the boss, and ask him for a recommendation. Always take the high road because it will establish nothing but respect for you. Don't seek revenge or try to sabotage the company. The best thing you can do is go out, find another job, and show the world that your previous employer made a huge mistake by letting you go.

# How Do I Find a New Job?

One of the first things we suggest you do is visit with your bishop. He can put you in touch with your ward employment specialist, who serves as your personal trainer. From there you can contact LDS Employment Services, which is full of highly trained professionals who can assist in your job search. LDS Employment Services offers free pamphlets, classes, and training. It is open to all, whether or not they are members of the Church.

In addition, seek help from family, friends, acquaintances, people you work with or have worked with, people you buy from, or professional organizations or clubs. We call this method *networking*. Sixty-five percent of all jobs are found through this method.

A second source for help is the source we most commonly think of when we are looking for employment—*want ads, agencies, and job postings*. Whereas 65 percent of all jobs are found from personal contact, 20 percent are found in this manner.

A third source of employment is the *Internet*. Ten percent of all employment opportunities are located on the Internet, and if you are in a computer field, that number jumps even higher. LDS Employment Services can provide you with a pamphlet featuring the most recent listings of Internet Web sites that can assist you in your job search.

Finally, 5 percent of all persons looking for work find jobs through making unsolicited, nonreferred calls to employers. This is called *cold calling*. Make a list of some of the places you would like to work, and speak to the human resources people or someone who works in a department that interests you. Ask for an "informational meeting" or just a personal conversation in which you might ask for advice. To reiterate, no one turns down an opportunity to give advice, and this could be your foot in the door.

The most important thing to remember when you are looking

for work is that you should not neglect any of these methods. Who knows which one will be the ticket to your new job? Though one method may traditionally yield more success than another, you do not know which one will land you the job of your dreams.

Let's go back to *networking* because it is often the most successful way to find work. The best thing about networking is that it gives you so many people to assist you in your search. What do we mean? Well, never has the majority of people in the United States been out of work at the same time. In recent history, unemployment seldom has risen above 5 percent, though it is higher during the current recession. So if 5 percent of us are out of work, then 95 percent of us are employed. Even in a bad economy when more people are out of work, that still leaves you a pretty good-sized pool of people who will help assist you in your job search.

Your network contact can be your neighbor, your best friend, your barber, your mailman, or even just someone you bump into in a grocery store. If you are helping someone else find a job, remember that you don't need to know of a job opening to help— all you need do to is put the person in touch with someone who works in the field of interest. Rarely will the person you contact know of a perfect employment match. But that person may know of someone who knows someone, who knows someone else, who *does know* where a job can be found.

The same goes for you in your search. When you meet *someone in your field,* make sure you keep in touch with that person as often as possible. *It is a mistake to assume that you are making a pest of yourself by making too frequent contacts. It only demonstrates your sincere interest.* Of course, you can stay too long or talk too much and inconvenience your contact, but a quick hello, the dropping off of a resume, and a friendly reminder that you are still looking for work keeps your name in your contact's mind. Because of these efforts, *you may become the first person your contact thinks of when a job comes along.*

Most everyone knows that their state employment office or a state department of workforce services will provide a complete listing of job opportunities registered with them. But did you also know that some television stations carry employment television programs with job listings? Check your television or cable provider for details. When you see a job listed that interests you, make contact as quickly as possible. A lot of people are looking for work at any given time, and the sooner you make contact the better—be the first one on the spot. Make your contact personal. Never mail your resume. You should always personally deliver the resume and say hello to the person doing the hiring. Then you should *follow up, follow up, follow up!*

In addition, do not overlook temporary agencies. Some businesses screen employees through temp agencies by trying them out on the job. If you are older than fifty, this can be one of your best sources of employment.

One of the best things you can do is *sharpen your interview skills and learn how to sell yourself.* Did you know that you should prepare and perfect a *thirty-second summary* of your positive points to best sell yourself and your employment skills? LDS Employment Services offers classes to both sharpen your interview skills and prepare your thirty-second summary. In addition, check with your county or state employment services to see what classes they offer on a low-cost or no-cost basis to improve these skills.

# Don't Give Up

These can be tough times, but answers can be obtained through help from friends, the Church, and the Lord. Don't be afraid to talk to your bishop or home teacher, and make sure you talk to your Heavenly Father. Fasting and prayer can also help open new and better doors of opportunity. Job security and satisfaction are essential to a family's happiness, and the breadwinner should always remember that tough financial times are hard on all members of the family. Consequently, this is a time for all to exercise faith.

Let's end where we began with a discussion of those bits of wisdom I learned from my dad. Our family was poor. We could have been considered down and out. As a family of five we lived in a two-room house, and my father moved from job to job trying to make ends meet. We did not have the luxury of having store-bought clothes, and we could never afford turkey for Thanksgiving. We lost everything in a nursery we had started when all the plants contracted a disease that wiped out our entire plant stock.

My folks never complained as I watched my father use his head *and* his hands. He taught us to "work harder than others." With his two hands and his imagination, he built for us a comfortable life. Many of you have experienced the same. What I learned most from my father and my mother was faith in God's help, hard work, and love for each other. We really never noticed what we didn't have. We did notice, however, what we did have, and that was a happy family. So can you.

PART FOUR

# Summing It Up

# Chapter 18

# Bent Nails and Clean Plates

On July 4, 1845, Henry David Thoreau embarked upon an experiment in living the simple life. He moved into a self-built house on land owned by his mentor, Ralph Waldo Emerson, on the shores of Walden Pond. There among the trees and within the sound of calling birds, he learned that "most of the luxuries, and many of the so-called comforts, of life are not only not indispensable, but positive hindrances to the elevation of mankind."[1]

Thoreau's reflections take me back to a day I (Lyle) still cherish. I was just a boy in those years, and my family was poor. I say that we were poor only with hindsight because I never thought so at the time. I lived like most of the other families in my neighborhood. I thought we lived like kings! I learned some valuable lessons in those years.

I was born in a small two-room house without running water or a bathroom. We took our baths on Saturday night in a double-sized washtub in the middle of the kitchen floor. We were concealed by a makeshift "modesty curtain" made out of old bedsheets that my mother hung on a line in front of the tub. If we had to answer the "call of nature," we made our way to the family outhouse. That outhouse was constructed by Works Progress Administration crews during the Great Depression, and my father always referred to it as the Roosevelt Monument.

Hard work was something you just learned in those days, and you learned it from the time you were old enough to fetch. Hard work and frugality went hand in hand. My father kept a bucket into which he would throw old, bent nails. He had bent these nails when he tried to hammer them, or pulled them from a discarded board or removed them from a broken piece of furniture. When he thought I needed to work, he called me to him, handed me the bucket of bent nails and a hammer, and said, "Your job is to straighten the nails. We don't waste a good nail." So by the hour I would straighten nails and put them into a second bucket of nails ready to be reused.

My father and mother's frugality extended far beyond the nail bucket. My dad kept a second bucket for old leftover screws from a repair job or project. We just didn't throw anything away if it still had a use. We kept good cardboard boxes, good milk cartons, glass jars—anything that might be used again. My mother sewed our clothes, saved fabric scraps for quilts or rugs, and kept all loose elastic bands, which were wrapped neatly around a plastic container in her kitchen "tool drawer."

Today I still maintain many of the habits of my parents. In my garage I have a screw bucket and a nail bucket. It is surprising, but hardly a week goes by that I don't need a screw or a nail from my bucket. My buckets keep me from wasting time and gasoline running to the store just to buy a few nails or a screw or two. I barely remember putting so many screws into my screw bucket, but year after year the amount keeps growing, and now it is filled to the brim. It has become a real money saver.

My mother extended this thrift to our family dinners. We had many lean times—times when there were more needs than money. I never remember once, however, ever leaving the table hungry. Many nights we dined on soup made from carefully saved bones from beef roast, roasted chicken, or turkey. On other nights, just before dinnertime, Mother would take from her oven six hot loaves of bread. We would feast that evening on bread and milk.

Everything my mother cooked was homemade, and she was a wonderful cook.

Today when I see restaurants advertise "homemade food," I have to chuckle. Somehow I can't imagine a chef bringing from home something he made in his kitchen to serve in his restaurant. When I watch young people dine out more often than they dine in, I feel sorry for them as I remember those wonderful meals my mother cooked. Young people do not realize that meals prepared at home cost much less and taste much better.

A recent trip to the grocery store set me to thinking about just how much we waste in today's throw-away world. I watched as a produce worker threw dozens of beautiful avocados into the garbage. When I asked him why, he told me that they were getting soft. I picked one up. It was ripe, precisely the way I liked it. I asked the man if I could buy these ripe avocados from him at a discount. "No," he said, "you will have to buy the harder ones and wait a few days for them to ripen."

For many decades, a disease of overabundance has plagued us. It has made us soft, and we have become proud. In our haughtiness we have forgotten that there are still some among us who are needy.

My mother always told us, "Don't take more than you can eat" and "Clean your plate." It was what every mother said in our day. My wife and I have tried to continue this legacy. Over the years, delicious stews and casseroles filled with leftover vegetables and meats have filled our table. We planted gardens, organized our refrigerators, and filled the shelves with home-canned goods.

That wonderful way of life has become nearly extinct. I remember a day not long ago when I overheard one of our sons say to my wife, "Mom, I don't eat leftovers. If I didn't eat it the first day, why would I want it the second day?" My son was reflecting the viewpoint of our day. He laughed and so did we, but it really wasn't funny. Bent nails and clean plates seem like wonderful relics worthy of rediscovery.

Perhaps the day of discovery is at hand. Economic instability came upon us suddenly and hit us hard without apparent warning. When it came, my mind immediately returned to a priesthood session of general conference. I heard, and so did you, President Gordon B. Hinckley warn us to get out of debt. "The time has come," he said, "to get our houses in order. . . . There is a portent of stormy weather ahead to which we had better give heed."[2]

In a day when his words of prophetic warning have been fulfilled, we can almost hear his cheery reply to those of us burdened with worry about our family's welfare. He would probably say something like this: "Brothers and sisters, isn't this a marvelous time to be alive?"

A marvelous time it truly is! This is the time we get to show what we are made of. This is the moment we've all waited for. This is the day when life got a whole lot simpler. We all have spent too much time trying to impress people with money we don't have, only to discover that those we thought we impressed really didn't care. So this day becomes a grand opportunity to put into practice those old rules for living we learned at our parents' knees.

A friend of ours writes his own memories of a time long ago, a time that seems like a reflection of our own day:

> I was born six months before Pearl Harbor and became the fruits of the Depression era and a very patriotic people. When I was a boy my father also had me pulling nails from used lumber and putting them in a can. Then my assignment was to pound them all straight.
>
> My father was a carpenter, and I barely knew how to use a hammer and saw (my left thumb still has a sawtooth scar to prove it). One summer day when I was nine, I loaded my wagon with scrap lumber and, with the can of used nails, I proceeded to build a house. My two younger sisters and I had many enjoyable playtime

hours in it. It weathered the storms for three more years when we moved away.

My father passed away at age eighty-three, and when I went to his shop to search through his treasures, I discovered a soup can full of rusty nails. I do not remember what else I salvaged, but I now have that can of rusty nails sitting on my desk, a symbol of what my father taught me about frugality and hard work.

Another Church member wrote of similar pleasant memories of her grandfather: "My mom told me about my grandpa who grew up during the Great Depression. She said that when she was cleaning out his workroom after he passed away, she came upon a drawer full of short string. The label read 'String—too short to use.' His generation simply used everything and wasted very little." This sister has adopted many of the same practices that made her grandfather such a wise patriarch. "Before I throw anything away, I look at it in a different light and think *Is there anything else this could be used for?* . . . Sometimes you just have to think broader."

The proverb "Waste not, want not" is still sound advice. In the coming years it will become not just our motto but also our temporal salvation. The goodness of this earth is a gift from a kind Father in Heaven. He commands us also to be wise stewards. He also commands us to provide for ourselves and our family, as well as for those who are less fortunate. In fulfilling the Lord's commandments, we learn to become more like him. It is then that the real blessings of heaven start to flow.

This truly *is* a marvelous time to be alive.

# Chapter 19

# What It Feels Like to Live a Full Life for Half the Price

We have come to the conclusion of *Live Your Life for Half the Price*. Together we have explored many cost-saving tips and governing rules for the control of our family economy. Perhaps you have incorporated some of these suggestions into your life. We hope you don't try to do too much too soon. It is vital that you make changes to your life slowly and consistently so that you do not become overwhelmed and abandon your resolve.

Taking control of our financial matters, particularly when we appeal to and follow the prophetic counsel we have been given, is an important part of finding peace and happiness in life.

In a First Presidency message that was published in March 1990, President Hinckley wrote:

> I wish to discuss a trap that can destroy any of us in our search for joy and happiness. It is that devious, sinister, evil influence that says, "What I have is not enough. I must have more." . . .
>
> Of course, we need to earn a living. The Lord told Adam that in the sweat of his face should he eat bread all the days of his life. It is important that we qualify ourselves to be self-reliant, particularly that every young man at the time of marriage be ready and able to assume

the responsibilities of providing for his companion and for the children who may come to that home.

Yet none of us ever has enough—at least that is what we think. No matter our financial circumstances, we want to improve them. This, too, is good if it is not carried to an extreme. . . .

It is when greed takes over, when we covet that which others have, that our affliction begins. And it can be a very sore and painful affliction. . . .

Be wise and do not go beyond your ability to pay. . . .

Said President Heber J. Grant: "If there is any one thing that will bring peace and contentment into the human heart, and into the family, it is to live within our means, and if there is any one thing that is grinding, and discouraging and disheartening it is to have debts and obligations that one cannot meet." (*Relief Society Magazine,* May 1932, p. 302)

It is the obsession with riches that cankers and destroys. The Lord has said: "Seek not for riches but for wisdom, and behold, the mysteries of God shall be unfolded unto you, and then shall you be made rich. Behold, he that hath eternal life is rich" (D&C 6:7).

As we go forward with our lives, let us remember the promise of the Lord: "Seek ye first the kingdom of God, and his righteousness; and all these things shall be added unto you" (Matt. 6:33). I bear testimony of the validity of that divine promise.[1]

We cannot say it better. To be rich in the things of eternity comes by putting our financial houses in order and seeking for the kingdom of God and his righteousness.

To live a full life, even when that life is paid for at half the cost of our former lifestyle, is rich and filled with peace and joy untold. Remember the governing rules from which you could learn to control your family's economy? Here they are again:

1. Love the Lord by living on faith in financial matters.

2. Let virtue garnish your thoughts, and obey the commandments of the Lord.

3. Cultivate a spirit of charity, particularly within your home.

4. Organize yourself and prepare every needful thing.

5. Seek not for riches but for wisdom.

Those rules have governed every principle and bit of advice we have offered you in this book.

Has your life improved? We hope so. Bickering over money matters has led to the greatest cause for divorce, but we hope you have developed a peace in your home you did not know before. Worry over money keeps many parents awake at night, but we hope you are sleeping more peacefully. Life can become overwhelming and circumstances can spiral beyond our control, but we hope you now feel a control over your family's destiny you hadn't felt before.

This life can be full without the things the world imagines are necessary for fulfillment. We hope you are on your way to achieving such a full life. May God bless you in your endeavors.

# Notes

## Introduction: A Penny Saved Is a Penny Earned

1. Tracy Connor, "Staten Island Woman Finds Streets Paved with Change," *New York Daily News,* January 12, 2009.
2. Available at www.globalrichlist.com.
3. Jean Chatzky, *You Don't Have to Be Rich: Comfort, Happiness, and Financial Security on Your Own Terms* (New York: Penguin Group, 2003), 129.
4. David Wallenchinsky, "Is the American Dream Still Possible?" *Parade,* April 23, 2006, 4–5.

## Chapter 1: The Secret to Living on Less

1. Gordon B. Hinckley, "To the Boys and to the Men," *Ensign,* November 1998, 52–53; emphasis added.
2. Quoted in Max Alexander, "Staying Ahead in Tough Times," *Reader's Digest,* August 2001, 86.

## Chapter 2: Putting a Price Tag on Happiness

1. David G. Myers, "Wanting More in an Age of Plenty," *Christianity Today,* April 24, 2000. Available at www.christianitytoday.com/ct/2000/april24/6.94.html.
2. BBC News, "Nigeria Tops Happiness Survey." Available at http://news.bbc.co.uk/2/hi/africa/3157570.stm.
3. Richard Ernsberger, "Behind the Smile," *Newsweek,* July 26, 2004.

4. David G. Myers, "The Secret to Happiness," *Yes!* magazine, Summer 2004, 13-16.

5. Ibid.

6. Ibid.

7. Matthew Herper, "Now It's a Fact: Money Doesn't Buy Happiness," *Forbes* magazine. Available only at http://moneycentral.msn.com/ content/invest/forbes/P95294.asp.

8. "More Sad Stories of Lottery Winners Ending Up Broke, Depressed and Lonely," *Life Two.* Available at http://lifetwo.com/production/ node/20070425-more-sad-stories-of-lottery-winners-ending-up-broke -depressed-and-lonely.

9. Myers, "Secret to Happiness."

10. BBC News, "Test Your Happiness." Available at http://news.bbc .co.uk/2/hi/programmes/happiness_formula/4785402.stm.

11. Myers, "Secret to Happiness."

12. Quoted in Claudia Dreifus, "The Smiling Professor," *New York Times,* April 22, 2008.

## Chapter 3: Do I Really Need This?

1. Alex Martin. Available at www.littlebrowndress.com.

2. Quoted in M. P. Dunleavey, "Getting Off the Spending Treadmill." Available at http://articles.moneycentral.msn.com/SavingandDebt/ SaveMoney/GetOffTheSpendingTreadmill.aspx?page=1.

3. Available at www.christianpf.com/10-free-household-budget -spreadsheets.

## Chapter 4: Family Fun on a Shoestring

1. Originally published in *Parent Magazine,* July 1949; reprinted in *30th Anniversary Reader's Digest Reader* (Pleasantville, N.Y.: Reader's Digest Association, 1951), 38–40. Available at http://www.infj.com/ ChickenSoup8.htm.

## Chapter 5: How to Avoid Starving to Death on Food

1. "Half of U.S. Food Goes to Waste." Available at www.foodproduction daily.com/Supply-Chain/half-of-US-food-goes-to-waste.

2. Ibid.

3. Rachel Oliver, "All About: Food Waste." Available at www.cnn .com/2007/WORLD/asiapcf/09/24/food.leftovers/#cnnSTCText.

4. Ibid.

5. Valerie Phillips, "Spoiled Rotten," *Deseret News,* February 25, 2009, C8.
6. See "Let's Eat Out: Americans Weigh Taste, Convenience, and Nutrition." Available at www.ers.usda.gov.
7. Available at www.restaurant.org/research.
8. "Frugal Lunch by Clever Dudette." Available at http://cleverdude .com/content/frugal.

## Chapter 6: How to Own a Home without Its Owning You

1. "'Mid Pleasures and Palaces," *Hymns* (Salt Lake City: The Church of Jesus Christ of Latter-day Saints, 1948), no. 185.
2. This family is a fictional composite of several real families.
3. "Other People's Money," *Reader's Digest,* June 2002, 192.
4. Available at www.faircredit.org/services_foreclosure.asp.

## Chapter 7: How to Keep the Lights On

1. Percentages calculated by Utah Power and Light, 2005.
2. Jane Bennet Clark, "29 Ways to Conserve and Save," *Kiplinger's Personal Finance,* October 2007. Available at www.kiplinger.com/ magazine/archives/2007/10/conserve.html.

## Chapter 8: How to Keep Your Car from Driving You to the Poorhouse

1. Dan Shapley, "10 Ways to Save Money on Gas," *The DailyGreen,* March 17, 2008. Available at http://www.thedailygreen.com/ environmental-new/latest/save-gas-47031702.

## Chapter 10: Having a Really Merry Christmas

1. See Charles D. Cohen, "The True Spirit of the Grinch," *Redbook,* December 1957.
2. Available at http://www.census.gov/Press-Release/www/releases/ archives/cb08ff-21.pdf.

## Chapter 11: Good Health Is like Cash in the Bank

1. Available at http://thinkexist.com/quotes/buddha/4.html.
2. Doug Trapp, "Health Insurance for the Unemployed Often Un-affordable," *American Medical News.* Available at www.ama-assn.org/ amednews/2009/01/19/gvsd0123.htm.

3. "Unemployed Workers Need Assistance Paying for Health Insurance; Only about One of Ten Obtain COBRA Coverage," January 27, 2009. Available at www.medicalnewstoday.com/articles/136704.php.

4. Lisa Nichols, "Buying Unemployed Medical Coverage," September 8, 2007. Available at http://health-insurance.suite101.com/article.cfm/buying_unemployed_medical_coverage.

5. Ibid.

## Chapter 12: The Benefits and Pitfalls of Insurance

1. N. Eldon Tanner, "Constancy amid Change," *Ensign,* November 1979, 82.

2. Available at www.merriam-webster.com.

3. Eric Tyson, *Personal Finance for Dummies* (3d ed., 2000), 337.

## Chapter 13: The Difference between Ants and Grasshoppers

1. Available at http://www.quotationspage.com/quote/2949.html.

2. Joseph Jacobs, *Aesop's Fables,* Harvard Classics series, vol. 17 (New York: P. F. Collier & Son, 1909–14), part 1.

3. Spencer W. Kimball, *The Teachings of Spencer W. Kimball* (Bookcraft, 1982), 353–54.

4. Ibid, 357–58.

## Chapter 14: Starving the Beast

1. Available at http://en.thinkexist.com/quotations/possessions/3.html.

2. Jay MacDonald, "You Might Be a Shopaholic If . . ." Available at http://www.bankrate.com/msn/news/advice/20030314a1.asp.

3. "What Is Spending Addiction, and How Do I Know if I Have It?" Available at www.4therapy.com/consumer/conditions/article/5686/566/what + Is + Spending + Addiction % 97And + How + Do + I + Know + If + I + Have + It % 3F.

4. Available at http://thinkexist.com/quotes/frederick_keonig.

## Chapter 15: Adjusting Your Income and Expenses in Turbulent Times

1. Available at http://en.thinkexist.com/quotes/maxwell_maltz/2.html.

2. Simran Khurana, "Henry David Thoreau Quote." Available at www

.quotations.about.com/od/stillmorefamouspeople/a/HenryDavid
Thor2.htm.

3. Fair Credit Foundation, "Debt Warning Signs." Available at www
.faircredit.org/warningsigns.asp.

4. Fair Credit Foundation. "Options and Strategies for Managing Debt."
Available at www.faircredit.org/options.asp.

5. "Stealing People Is Wrong," *Economist,* March 8, 2001.

6. Suggestions from Division of Consumer Protection and Federal
Trade Commission.

7. "Discover Card Privacy Policy," copyright 2009 Discover Bank
PRVCY09. Available at www.discovercard.com/discover/data/customer/
faq/privacypolicy.shtml#top.

8. Gordon B. Hinckley, "To the Boys and to the Men," *Ensign,* November 1998, 51.

## Chapter 16: Financial Fidelity

1. Richard Alan Krieger, *Civilization's Quotations* (Algora Publishing, 2002), 264. Available at http://thinkexist.com/quotes/
louis_k._anspacher.

2. Karen Sherman, "MSN Money," April 8, 2008.

3. N. Eldon Tanner, "Constancy amid Change," *Ensign,* November
1979, 80.

## Chapter 17: Coping with Unemployment and Underemployment

1. Available at http://quotations.about.com/cs/inspirationquotes/a/
Attitude15.htm.

2. Steven Jobs, commencement address, Stanford University, June 12,
2005.

3. Ibid.

4. Brent D. Peterson and Gaylan W. Nelson, *Fake Work: Why People Are
Working Harder Than Ever but Accomplishing Less, and How* (New
York: Simon Spotlight Entertainment, 2009), 3.

5. Kay Bell, "Tax Help after a Layoff," January 2009. Available at www
.bankrate.com//finance/money-guides/tax-help-after-a-layoff-1.aspx.

## Chapter 18: Bent Nails and Clean Plates

1. Henry David Thoreau, *Walden* (New York: Longmans, Green and
Co., 1910), 12.

2. Gordon B. Hinckley, "To the Boys and to the Men," *Ensign,* November 1998, 53.

## Chapter 19: What It Feels Like to Live a Full Life for Half the Price

1. Gordon B. Hinckley, "Thou Shalt Not Covet," *Ensign,* March 1990, 2–5.

# Index

# Index

# About the Authors

Lyle and Tracy Shamo have made a lifelong habit of debt management and stretching household dollars. Lyle has been a frequent lecturer on this subject to bank and credit union clients, Church groups, and other community gatherings throughout Utah and Idaho. Tracy has frequently discussed household finances on a Salt Lake City radio station.

The Shamos now reside in England, where Lyle is serving as president of the London South Mission of The Church of Jesus Christ of Latter-day Saints. He previously served as a bishop (twice), a member of four stake presidencies, high councilor, ward Young Men's president, elders quorum president, and a teacher (numerous times). Recently retired, Lyle served as an instructor at the Salt Lake Institute of Religion and was formerly the managing director of the Church's Audiovisual Department. He holds a bachelor's degree in speech and public address and a master's degree in instructional science and media, both from Brigham Young University.

Tracy is a homemaker. She holds a bachelor's degree in speech and dramatic arts from Brigham Young University and is the author of numerous scripts for Church movies and videos. She also served as co-host of "Concerts from Temple Square," a radio program of music produced by the Church. Tracy has served in many Church callings and especially enjoys those that involve teaching. She and Lyle are the parents of eight and grandparents of thirteen.